GRAND PRIX

GRAND PRIX

The Complete Book of Formula 1 Racing

Text by Elizabeth Hayward
Photographs by David Phipps

Produced by Lyle Kenyon Engel
and the Editors of Auto Racing Magazine

DODD, MEAD & COMPANY · NEW YORK

The following supplementary photography is hereby gratefully acknowledged: Geoffrey Goddard: pages 129, 130, 135 left, 137, 140, 145 left, 146 left, 149, 156, 166, 167, 168; Eric della Faille: pages 12-13; Larry D. Kincaid: page 128. The photograph on page 138 is reprinted through the courtesy of René Dreyfus.

ISBN: 0-396-06418-3

Library of Congress Catalog Card Number: 75-169731

Printed in the United States of America

INTRODUCTION

TO "GET a Formula 1 drive" is the ultimate dream of every young racing driver I've ever met—at least on the European side of the Atlantic. The fact that I am solely concerned with Grand Prix racing and that, out of thirteen Grands Prix each year all but four at present take place in Europe, must be kept in mind when you read this book. My view of the scene is a very personal one, simply because I am committed to go wherever the Grand Prix "circus" goes; at the beginning of March we fly out to South Africa and from then till Mexico at the end of October we have a Grand Prix almost every other weekend, with a few non-Championship Formula 1 races before and during the season to keep everyone on his toes.

The drivers, constructors, entrants and mechanics are my friends—the only ones I ever have time to make, because between races I'm either writing about them or going to see new cars being built or attending functions where we all meet yet again. I wouldn't have it any other way. The people in motor racing are the most intelligent, the most entertaining, the most complex and the most rewarding, in the way of mental stimulation, that I've met since I left art college many years ago. Because we all share the same interests, face the same heartaches and live so much of our lives together, we are a close-knit group and necessarily emotionally involved.

Some writers prefer to steer clear of "getting involved"; by which they mean that they never allow themselves to become too friendly with a racing driver in case he gets killed and they have their feelings hurt. I think they miss a great deal. All the top drivers have a zest for living and a talent for packing an enormous amount of experience into every day. They pass on this sense of "life is meant for living," plus something of their unique personalities, which I consider one of the most important reasons for leading this mad, itinerant existence. My life, for instance, would have been infinitely poorer if I had *not* known Bruce McLaren, Jim Clark, Wolfgang von Trips, Jochen Rindt. It was agony to lose them, but it was wonderful knowing them.

The cars in Formula 1 racing can also be the objects of affection and despair, though on a very different level. They are like thoroughbred race horses; highly strung, sleek, fast, sometimes temperamental, mostly beautiful. They are the product of years of thought and development, of flashes of genius fired with solid engineering knowledge. The designers are specialized, often with previous experience in the aircraft industry. The constructors (who are in some cases also the designers) are a mixed bunch, outwardly, but some of them have raced cars in their time and are, or have been, engineers as well. They each have their own philosophy, their own vision of what a racing car should be—these vary considerably.

The mechanics are a race apart; they are incredibly dedicated to their job, they almost ruin their lives to make racing cars and keep them running, and yet, in some cases, they do not like motor racing itself. For them the satisfaction is in the messy, underpaid, extremely hard and uncomfortable work they do. They have my unstinted admiration.

Many, many other people go into the running of each Grand

Prix—the tire companies and their personnel, the component manufacturers, the sponsors, the organizers, the timekeepers, the marshals, the team managers, the secretaries back at the factories. I've tried to cover every facet of Formula 1 motor racing in this book as thoroughly as I can in the space available. I've tried to give you an idea of what it is like to be a member of the "circus," with its triumphs and disasters and even its petty irritations. It is a way of life (one on which I seem to be "hooked," although it apparently runs contrary to my background, taste and training); I hope I can give you something of its unique flavor in these few chapters.

To cover all thirteen Grands Prix at present on the calendar, I travel about fifty thousand miles a year. A racing driver travels a great deal more, especially if he runs in Can-Am or the World Sports Car Manufacturers' Championship races as well, but he can usually afford it more easily than a journalist! Travel is expensive, rather tedious at times, especially a night flight across the Atlantic, and yet I get a very restless feeling every time I hear a jet plane over our home on its final run into London Airport. The truth is, I can scarcely contain my impatience to start the new season —which takes us to the first Grand Prix of the year, South Africa, then on to Spain, Monaco, Belgium, Holland, France, Great Britain, Germany, Austria, Italy, Canada, the United States and Mexico.

ELIZABETH HAYWARD

CONTENTS

GRAND PRIX

FORMULA 1

FORMULA 1 MOTOR RACING is the top of
a large tree with many branches; its roots, in
Europe at least, grow in the fertile ground of
club racing, a sport for anyone with the in-
clination and with a modicum of cash to buy a Lotus 7 or a second-
hand Mini or two-seater sports car. Almost all the top drivers in
the world today started their careers in decidedly second-hand
machinery, and several on motorcycles. The rich amateur whose
father bought him a brand-new racing car to start his career is
nearly a myth nowadays. Young drivers who show their merit in
club racing usually graduate, by their own efforts and savings, to
a Formula Ford, Formula Vee or Formula 3 car if they are truly
serious. If they have talent and begin to win races, established
teams will cast a benevolent but shrewd eye over them and perhaps
suggest a regular team drive.

This is the starting point for the long climb to the top, which is

**Jochen Rindt leads Jack Brabham (who is following so closely that
his car can barely be seen) during the 1970 British Grand Prix,
which Rindt won.**

1

Grand Prix racing, and some never progress beyond a Formula 3 team drive. Skill is needed, but so are luck and a steely determination. If you are in the right place at the right time you may be noticed by Ken Tyrrell, or Colin Chapman, or Ron Tauranac, or one of the other well-known talent spotters. If there is a drive going begging, you may be asked to fill the vacant seat for a trial period. If you make good in the first year—by which I mean if you put up some good practice times, are consistently never farther than half-way down the grid and collect the odd championship point—then you are IN. You will be one of those few drivers (about twenty-five at the present time) who reach the summit of their profession, and will take part in the series of Grands Prix from which only one man each year can emerge with the title "World Champion."

So what *is* Formula 1? Why should the world champion racing driver come from these ranks alone?

Weird-looking "wings" on Jacky Ickx's Brabham Ford at the 1969 Spanish Grand Prix. The rear wing is already buckled and later it failed completely.

Aerodynamic aids at the front end of the 1969 Matra MS80 Ford included vertical "fences" in addition to the more normal dive fins.

For the answers we have to go back a long way—to France in the latter years of the last century. The first motoring events took place on ordinary roads, drivers of all calibers taking their vehicles, which were of all and any type, from one town to another as fast as they could. At first they were more reliability runs than races but, naturally, it wasn't long before engineers were using all their ingenuity and skill to make their own particular charger go faster than the others. For the most part, the men who drove the cars were the makers themselves, and the steam-versus-internal-combustion controversy was being fought out as an exercise in reliability and speed.

Names like Peugeot, Panhard and Levassor, Daimler and Benz, de Dion and Bouton are so much a part of our everyday motoring vocabulary that we have forgotten their origins. They were inventors, pioneers, competitors, partners and sometimes protagonists.

In 1887 there were two local "runs" in the environs of Paris. The first was a walkaway by Georges Bouton driving a de Dion tricycle—he was the only starter! Later in the year there was a slightly more ambitious venture, a run for steam vehicles from Paris to Versailles, about twenty miles. A steam tricycle built by Bouton was the first to arrive, but either he did not see or chose to ignore the control, and continued much farther. The prize therefore went to his partner, the Marquis Albert de Dion (one of the most enthusiastic founders of motoring as a sport) who was driving a brand-new quadricycle.

Chris Amon, Jack Brabham, Jean-Pierre Beltoise, Jacky Ickx, Denis Hulme and Henri Pescarolo play follow the leader as they rush out of the Chicane and down to the Tobacconist's Corner during the 1970 Grand Prix of Monaco.

In 1894 there was the first of the famous runs, actually a "Concours" sponsored by the Paris newspaper *Le Petit Journal*. This was more of a rally than anything else, with trucks, buses, steam-

and gasoline-powered cars, et al. The factories of Peugeot and Panhard were awarded equal first prizes, the cars using Daimler engines. And a year later came the world's first *real* motor *race,* the Paris-Bordeaux-Paris.

This attracted a large and varied entry, and the prize money was over $5000. This was to be a pure speed race, and it was won by Emile Levassor on his two-seater Panhard-Phénix in 48 hours 48 minutes. Unfortunately, only four-seaters qualified for prize money, and a Peugeot-Daimler, exactly 11 hours behind, collected the top prize. This event made quite an impact on the public, and was certainly a landmark for the sport.

(The first American road race was run a few months later near Chicago, with six starters and two finishers, an American Duryea and a Benz.)

After that races were organized, if you can use that word seriously, all over Europe—except in England, where motor racing on public roads has always been illegal. The cars became more powerful and the crowds grew bigger for each event. The horseless carriage was still a thing of great wonder among all but the rich and fanatical. The Gordon Bennett Challenge Trophy races began in

Jacky Ickx's Ferrari leads Jean-Pierre Beltoise's Matra over a bridge at Clermont-Ferrand. (1970 French GP)

1900 and lasted for five years, and during that time the gap between the ordinary road car and the specially built racing car became wider and wider. The disastrous Paris-Madrid race in 1903, in which spectators and competitors were killed, caused the French government to stop town-to-town racing altogether. Instead, with the supremacy of French machinery being at stake, they arranged for roads to be closed to form circuits, as Rouen, Clermont-Ferrand and so on are today.

It was in 1906 that the Automobile Club of France thought up the "Grand Prix" as we know it now. A "formula" was imposed: a set of rules, changed from time to time, setting limits to size, weight, engine capacity and such-like. Thus the French, unwittingly perhaps, began something which time and development have largely taken out of their hands. (But it is significant that the governing body of motor sport today, the Fédération Internationale de l'Automobile formed in 1904, is still a French originated, French language organization. The branch of the FIA which controls strictly sporting activities, i.e. racing, is the Commission Sportive Internationale, the CSI.)

From 1906 until the outbreak of the First World War in 1914 the French held an annual Grand Prix which became *the* great classic race of Europe. It turned into a battle between France, Germany and Italy, and the engines reached capacities of 16 liters in 1907 and 14 liters in 1912. Things were getting out of hand, so the formula set a maximum $4\frac{1}{2}$-liter engine capacity in 1914, the first regulation of its kind, and since then there has been strict adherence to some kind of capacity limit. In 1914 the German Mercedes-Benz team was all-conquering.

The war put an end to such frivolities as motor racing, and when it began again in Europe in 1921 the Germans were not allowed to take part. Each interested country now established its own Grand Prix; Italy first, then Spain, Monaco, Great Britain and Belgium. The Germans held their own sports car race each year, but re-entered international racing in 1934. It was to become a Fascist show window, and a very successful one.

Graham Hill surveys the remains of his Lotus Ford, which crashed after the rear wing collapsed during the 1969 Spanish Grand Prix. Following this race, suspension-mounted wings were banned.

Names like Fiat, Sunbeam, Bugatti, Alfa Romeo and Delage now made the headlines. Grand Prix speeds in 1924 were as high as 140 miles an hour, tires were skinny, the machines high off the ground, the cockpits wide open, the driver unprotected except for his goggles and maybe a leather helmet. Films of these long-ago races make hilarious viewing now, with the wild spins, the Mack Sennet-type pit stops and the encroaching crowds, but they must have been hair-raising at the time. The story of these times, and the remarkable engines and engineering to be seen and heard, have made whole books on their own. I haven't room to go into details, but it strikes me upon reading the history of motor racing how little new there is under the sun—or the hood.

The CSI came into being in 1922, and from that day to this has exercised its "Sporting Power" throughout the world. It revises the International Sporting Code periodically, draws up the sporting calendar for the coming year and the sporting regulations which are subject to yearly amendments. It also sees that these regulations are properly distributed, gives guidance on how to interpret them and sees that they are adhered to. It has delegates from the

automobile clubs of eighteen countries, holds two meetings annually, plus meetings of a smaller body, the "Bureau," which
gathers whenever necessary to decide urgent matters.

Currently, it decrees that in Formula 1 the engine capacity must
not exceed 3 liters unsupercharged and must use commercial fuel.
The car should have a minimum weight of 1162 pounds. The dis-
tance to be run for a Formula 1 event must be at least 300 kilome-
ters and not more than 400. These rules were instituted in 1966
and were supposed to come to an end in 1972, but they have been
granted an extension until 1975.

Over the years the rules have been changed frequently, and have
always caused an outcry of some sort or another. This is usually
unfair, because most of the changes have been made to keep racing
exciting, have served to promote the constructors' ingenuity, and
to proceed toward the supposed "ultimate" in racing machines.
The last Formula 1, which lasted from 1961 to the end of 1965,
dictated an engine capacity of not more than 1½ liters. Then
chassis and suspension improved so much, and tires held the road
so much better, that the cars were in advance of their engine power.
Thus the limit was raised to 3 liters unsupercharged (or 1½ liters
supercharged), which has already given us five years of close, exciting racing, with the initial supremacy of the Repco V8 being
overtaken by the astoundingly successful Ford Cosworth V8. It
wasn't until the latter part of 1970 that the 12-cylinder engines
began to show their long-promised potential.

So it is *history* which has given prime importance to the Grands
Prix and to Formula 1. Other types of motor racing were hardly
considered before the 1950s—Indianapolis was the only rival to
Formula 1, and that seemed a very long way from Europe until
1961 when Jack Brabham invaded the famous oval with his
strange, rear-engined, tiny Cooper. Now we have prototype sports
cars (Group 6), two-seater racing cars (Group 7—Can Am) and
all other Groups from 1 to 9, of which number 8 includes Formula
1, the open-wheel single-seater, the sophisticated aristocrat of motor
racing.

Another product of wing failure — Jochen Rindt's Lotus Ford, which crashed moments after teammate Hill's accident at the same place on the track. Rindt was not seriously injured and was soon racing again. (1969 Spanish GP)

In official parlance, they are "cars manufactured solely for speed races on a circuit or closed course," which also applies to F/2 and F/3. This gives you no idea of the enormous weight of prestige that Formula 1 carries as a result of its ancestry. One of the most important historical reasons for the supremacy of this formula is, rather ironically, the emphasis which was placed on this form of sport by Nazi Germany and Fascist Italy in the thirties. Hitler made no secret of the fact that he regarded German domination in this field as an expression of the potential domination of Germany itself. After the 1914-18 war and the defeat of his nation by the Allies, Hitler was not alone in wanting to prove to the world that Germany's engineering was a force to reckon with. Cars could become fighting and bombing aircraft, the team spirit shown on the race track could work in another direction too.

Germany returned to Grand Prix racing in 1934 with the start of a new formula—"the 750 kilogram formula," limiting cars to a weight of around 1654 pounds. Top speeds were expected to be in the 160-mph region. Both Mercedes-Benz and Auto-Union were ready, and it is interesting to note that Auto-Union used a V16 engine mounted behind the driver. (Designer, Dr. Ferdinand Porsche.) These firms were government sponsored and Hitler even went to great expense and trouble to have the Nürburgring built. He wanted it to be the most difficult circuit in the world so that he could show off "his" racing cars to their best advantage.

He succeeded. And with the success of the cars, the idea of a racing driver as a separate type of being was somehow born. Call it a cult, if you like; it still exists. Rudolph Caracciola, Manfred von Brauchitsh, Hermann Lang and Dick Seaman were to join the brilliant list of Mercedes drivers, while Auto-Union had Bernd Rosemeyer and Achille Varzi. Tazio Nuvolari, who started with Alfa Romeo and scored legendary victories, moved on to Auto-Union. A list of drivers of the twenties and thirties reads like an index of myths and legends. Was it any wonder that after the Second World War the sport of motor racing should draw into it some of the most skillful men the world has ever seen? Farina, Fangio, Ascari, Villoresi, Taruffi, Gonzalez, Hawthorn, Trintignant, Moss, Bira, Musso, Behra, Collins, de Portago, Flockhart, Schell, Brooks, von Trips, Lewis Evans, Salvadori—the list up to 1959 contains all these names, the races dominated by Fangio, Moss, Collins and Hawthorn. In 1958 we come across three new names—Brabham, Phil Hill and Graham Hill, all of which link us with the present day.

The cars were just as illustrious—Alfa Romeo, Maserati, Ferrari, Mercedes, BRM, Vanwall, Cooper and Lotus—products of brilliant engineering, the best that could be designed within each set of FIA rules at the time.

So Formula 1 Grand Prix racing has built and kept its magic, and remains the goal for all who want to be involved in what is simply the pinnacle of the sport—a kaleidoscopic, sometimes frantic, worldwide tour as drivers and constructors dash from country to country in search of the elusive title "World Champion."

THE DRIVERS

GRAND PRIX DRIVERS are a select group of maybe twenty men of widely differing nationalities, tastes and backgrounds, yet all with certain essential things in common. Over the years I have talked in ordinary conversation and in interviews on tape to virtually all the Grand Prix drivers from Stirling Moss to our newest recruits, François Cevert and his contemporaries. I have traveled with them, shared meals with them, watched them at work and at home, timed them in practice, noted their temperaments, their achievements, their failures and their behavior under almost all circumstances, including the death of friends.

For these years and for these relationships I am very grateful. They have given me an understanding of what being a racing driver *is,* and why it is so difficult to stop being one by choice. They have given me international values instead of parochial ones, and I have an enormous respect for the motivations of the world's best drivers.

I often find myself in frustrating argument with people who think all racing drivers must be out of their minds, or simply so selfish, greedy and belligerent that they cannot find a better way of satisfying their incredible urge to hurtle through the air at high speed, than climbing into a four-wheeled gasoline-tank and throwing it into near-impossible situations.

A lot of these anti-motor-racing campaigners are doctors, who spend almost all their lives trying to patch people up when they have been hurt or damaged through no fault of their own. It is not unnatural for them to view racing as a form of calculated suicide; but they don't understand.

Some people think drivers are exhibitionists, super-egotists, compensating for inadequacies in their characters, money-mad. All right, I'll go along with some of those, some of the way, with reference to some of the men involved. Most drivers like the cheers of the crowds and the laurel wreaths and the kisses of the pretty girls; but those same drivers are even happier on a deserted track testing a new car and taking it to limits they still have to assess.

Yes, I suppose you have to call them egotists. The potent combination of speed, skill, stamina, rewards, satisfaction in a job well done and the constant battle against all the forces that are working to drag you off a track, produce a feeling of exhilaration you cannot get in many other ways—it is a power game. Comparisons have been made with bullfighters, mountaineers, explorers, lone yachtsmen and trapeze artists. I think the nearest comparison it is

Rare group photo taken at the 1969 French GP: From left to right: Bruce McLaren, Denis Hulme, Graham Hill, Silvio Moser, Jo Siffert,

possible to make is between today's Grand Prix racing drivers and the pilots of the fantastic Red Arrows (RAF) aerobatics team. The U.S. Air Force probably has an equivalent. It is not insignificant that most of today's top drivers have been aloft with the Red Arrows—and been suitable scared! In return, the leader of the Red Arrows has said that nothing on earth would get him into a Grand Prix car—he feels there is a bit more room in the sky.

If the drivers do have character inadequacies or "hang-ups" which make them turn to this particular sport, I haven't seen much evidence of it. They are impatient of nine-to-five jobs and that "guaranteed pension" way of thinking; and they are restless. Some of them feed the press with a line about wanting to "spend more time with the family," and so on—well, after about two days at home there isn't one I know who isn't ready to be on the move again—testing tires, running a new car for the first time, tying up a business deal, flying off to a race.

Money is incidental. Money comes in fair-sized quantities only *after* you have proved yourself to have the necessary qualities. Even then, it doesn't always make you rich—a lot of people get a lot richer sitting in an office and picking up the telephone. Certainly, they'll say, it's nice to have money. They like the luxury side of Grand Prix racing, and the more money comes in the more

Jackie Stewart, and unknown spectator, Piers Courage, Jochen Rindt, Vic Elford, Jean-Pierre Beltoise, Jacky Ickx and Chris Amon.

13

1970 World Driving Champion Jochen Rindt at the wheel of the Lotus 49C Ford. (Monaco 1970)

they tend to want, like most human beings. But they are in the sport for reasons dictated mainly by their temperament, and a little by their early circumstances.

For a racing driver to reach the top bracket, he must have stamina, excellent eyesight, unusually fast reflexes and a bit more than ordinary physical fitness. He must be able to hold a car steady when enormous forces are pulling it another way, which needs strong arms and shoulders. He must be able to concentrate for hours at a time, and I mean *concentrate*. Even the tiniest mistake at 170 mph can mean disaster. Taking the same corner maybe 150, even 200 times in the course of one race meeting spread over three days, he must be able to choose a good line, and stick to it—hazards permitting—without deviating more than an inch or two.

He must possess an extraordinarily delicate sense of balance—usually called "driving through the seat of the pants"; and this, I think, is one of the greatest assets a driver can possess. The other

14

one is an even temperament in the face of disappointment. Obviously, a man may be speechless with frustration when his car breaks down on the last lap. He probably feels very sick and upset; but he mustn't stay that way for long. If he is not able to look disappointment straight in the eye and come to terms with it, thinking ahead philosophically to the next race, then he won't last long in the Grand Prix circus. Or if he stays in racing because of his skill, but without the right temperament to go with it, he will never be a champion. He will always imagine that the grass is greener in some other team, and move into a different stable just at the wrong moment. A good driver simply *has* to be able to keep his sense of humor—or at least his "cool"—whatever the circumstances.

The other obvious characteristics of a Grand Prix driver are a certain amount of "tiger" or aggressive spirit and an unquenchable competitive urge. Most top drivers compete in all sorts of areas, not only on the track. Most take up either golf, skiing, bobsleding, shooting, sailing, power-boating, flying, water-skiing—or womanizing; even making more money out of a business deal than the next man. It is all grist for the mill.

I never like to use the word "brave" in connection with racing drivers. They don't look upon themselves as particularly brave people. Determined they are, certainly, and less likely to give up in the face of adversity than you or I. But courage doesn't really enter into it. *They* would call being brave being stupid or foolhardy. No, it is more a determination not to be beaten by anything, not even injuries; because if for one moment they allowed themselves the luxury of self-pity, they would no longer be good racing drivers.

Alert, aware, philosophical, relaxed, confident and physically fit—that is quite a list of attributes, but a great driver needs them all. Intelligence of a high order goes without saying. A man who has to make split-second decisions, who needs to understand the behavior of his car as well as he understands his own body, who can memorize a completely new circuit within a few laps, that is an intelligent man.

Jacky Ickx captured three firsts, a second, a third and a fourth place finish to place second in the 1970 point standings.

1969 World Driving Champion Jackie Stewart had a less favorable season in 1970, finishing fifth in the standings.

Of the drivers taking part in the Grands Prix in 1970, we lost three of the very best—Bruce McLaren, Piers Courage and Jochen Rindt. The shock still reverberates through the circus, and the prospect of sudden death can never be ignored, of course. But none of us ever dwell on it. The driver knows, we all know, as we watch him drive out of the pits on any day of testing or practice or in the race, that we might never see him again. But we don't sit there brooding about it. The driver begins working out his line for the first corner, and we all set about our various tasks—timing, changing an engine or a gearbox, stacking some wet-weather tires or whatever.

Drivers are often asked if they are affected by seeing another driver crash, maybe fatally. Well, of course they are affected! What a silly question. Any driver's instinct might be to stop and help, but he knows there are plenty of people, marshals and ambulancemen and so on, who are stationed around the track for the very purpose of helping. So he goes on driving his race and his lap times don't fall off. He may even drive better, with a controlled anger against fate, and go on to win.

Things are a little different if an accident takes place during practice. If it appears to be a minor matter—and the drivers certainly take a very good look as they pass the scene to ascertain the state of affairs—they will make signals to the appropriate pit as they go by and press on for a quick lap. If, however, things look bad, or if there is debris on the track, they will come into the pits, have a quiet word with the mechanics and team manager concerned, and then wait in their own pit for news. The circuit will go quiet as the cars come in. And that is the most unpleasant time of all.

I remember the mingling of joy and pride and sadness which was manifest on Jacky Ickx's face when he won the French Grand Prix at Rouen in 1968, Ferrari's first victory since Monza two years before, and twenty-three-year old Jacky's first Grand Prix win. But what a disastrous race, with the death of Jo Schlesser, the popular French driver, in an uncontrollable fire in his Honda, and the number of pit stops arising from the fact that the other cars had to drive over bits of the wreckage. Jacky is a sensitive person, as well as fiercely competitive, and here was his greatest moment embittered and spoiled.

Jochen Rindt's first—and anxiously awaited—Grand Prix victory was almost as much a mixed-feelings affair. He won the U.S. Grand Prix in 1969 after a season of great promise and many disappointments, knowing that his teammate, Graham Hill, had suffered a very serious accident in the latter half of the race. He wouldn't accept congratulations or champagne or laurels until he had ascertained that Graham was, if much battered, at least unbowed.

Jochen's second victory the following year was utterly ruined for him when he learned that his great friend, Piers Courage, had died in the fire which destroyed his car in the Dutch Grand Prix. He received his laurels with tears in his eyes, and although he was to go on to more victories, he was never quite the same carefree young man I had previously known.

There are many examples of this tragedy all drivers have to face; Jackie Stewart had to go through the same thing at Monza when Jochen himself was killed. But anyone who thinks other people's accidents make a driver slower, more cautious, or influence him into retiring are wrong. A sadder, more mature man emerges from these disasters, maybe. Certainly none is quite the same again. But the professional Grand Prix driver will always carry on with his job, no matter how much he'd like to go away and hide in a corner, just because he is a professional, and there is a public waiting to see him drive; plus the knowledge that his dead comrade would think him a feeble creature if he acted any other way.

So don't ever ask a driver how he feels about another driver's accident or death. It is certain that he is deeply affected, stunned perhaps, but his best cure is to go out and drive—not necessarily more quickly or wildly, or more slowly, but just as well as he knows how. And it may take him days or weeks before he can talk about it objectively, though that depends on the individual.

There is no set pattern in a driver's background which throws up a "super-star," although there are some likenesses. Whatever the nationality (and we have Grand Prix drivers now from eleven different countries) most will have had a rather bad school record. From the most respectable, not to say conventional homes, have come these young men who were the despair of their teachers. The only subjects they showed interest in, if they were at that kind of school, were math and engineering drawing, or metalwork. Those who were expected to be academic, like Rindt, Ickx, Stewart, Courage and Cevert, were to prove disappointing to their elders at the age of fifteen or sixteen, only to find suddenly that there was something they were better at than anyone else—controlling a motorcycle or a car. The rest, I think I can say fairly, were never really expected to be scholastic. Even Bruce McLaren, who went on to study engineering at a university, was told by his teacher to choose between engineering and motor racing. Bruce used to say he'd chosen both, but he left the university without a degree.

Almost all of them learned to drive when very young, some on farms, like Jim Clark and Chris Amon, where father let them get to the wheel of a tractor early; some on motorcycles, like John Surtees, Jean-Pierre Beltoise and Jacky Ickx, all of whom rapidly progressed to four wheels; some picked up the knack while sitting on Dad's lap at the wheel of a car, like Denny Hulme, Jack Brabham and Bruce McLaren; some because Dad was in the garage business anyway, or took part in motoring sport himself. Of my acquaintance, only Graham Hill had not driven a car before he was in his twenties, but even he had had a go at motorcycle scrambling, and it was only lack of finance which delayed his start on cars. Hulme and Beltoise cut their teeth on trucks and Ickx on Army tanks!

Family wealth plays a very small part in forming the Grand Prix driver. Chris Amon, Jochen Rindt and Pedro Rodriguez have been exceptions, but most drivers have had a long, hard and expensive struggle simply to get near their first racing car. And even with parental help, in order to make the top rungs of the sport *every* driver has had to overcome either poverty, discouragement at home, lack of opportunities to drive competitively, being dubbed "a mechanic" and thus pigeon-holed, or the corroding influence of bad luck. Each driver deserves a chapter to himself, if not a whole book, but here, in less than a nutshell, are the backgrounds of those who were the top twenty Grand Prix drivers of 1970.

Amon, Chris—born New Zealand, 1943, son of a wealthy sheep farmer. Drove farm trucks at eleven, learned to fly at fifteen, racing cars at sixteen. Brilliant driver, especially for Ferrari (1967-69) and March (1970). Now going to Matra. Never won a Grand Prix.

Beltoise, Jean-Pierre—born Paris, France, 1937, son of a butcher, two years at engineering school, then motorcycle champion. Drove delivery vans in Paris. French Army private, wrote in spare time. Sports cars and F/2. Badly burned in Reims 12-hours in 1964. Matra Formula 3. Formula 2 Champion 1968. Matra Formula 1 1968-70. Never won a Grand Prix.

Brabham, John Arthur (Jack)—born Sydney Australia, 1926. Son of a greengrocer, became a garage mechanic. RAAF as a flight mechanic during part of Second World War, speedway midget racing from 1946. Built, tuned, raced cars, learned art and craft of racing. Drove for Cooper 1955-1961. World Champion 1959 and 1960. Formed Motor Racing Developments with Ron Tauranac in 1961, began to build Brabhams. Took World Championship in his own car 1966, always among the top four drivers. Retired after Mexican GP 1970.

Cevert, François—born Paris, 1944, son of wealthy Parisian jeweler. Sister Jacqueline married to Beltoise. Formula 3 Alpine 1967, Tecno 1968, French F/2 Champion. To Formula 1 in one leap 1970 when Johnny Servoz-Gavin retired from the Tyrrell team after Monaco. Has shown immense promise in first season in F/1, driving Tyrrell March Ford, should be even better in 1971 in Tyrrell Ford.

Courage, Piers, 1942-1970—born Colchester, England, eldest son

Chris Amon

Henri Pescarolo   Jackie Oliver

Piers Courage   **Rolf Stommelen**

of rich brewery owner. Schooling at Eton, trained as accountant, turned to racing originally for fun, became very professional. Never drove for big works team with any success, became top class as privateer with Frank Williams. Killed Dutch Grand Prix 1970.

Fittipaldi, Emerson—born Brazil, 1947. Kart and motorcycle racing at fifteen. Meteoric career in Brazilian motor racing, Formula 2 in England 1969 for Lotus, put into third Gold Leaf Team Lotus at British Grand Prix July 1970. Won first Grand Prix Watkins Glen October 1970! Racing with Lotus 1971.

Hill, Graham—born London, 1929, son of stockbroker. Out of work after naval service and apprenticeship at S. Smith & Sons (instrument manufacturers), begged drives in any car, any meeting. Had one driving lesson. Became mechanic with Team Lotus 1954, nagged Chapman into letting him drive a works car, 1956.

22

Formula 1 Lotus 1958-59, then joined BRM and stayed for seven years. World Champion 1962. Returned to Lotus 1967, World Champion 1968. Bad crash United States GP 1969, made determined recovery, drove Lotus for Rob Walker 1970.

Hulme, Denis—born Nelson, New Zealand, 1936. Drove trucks for father's haulage business from early age, first raced MG 1956. Came to England under "Driver to Europe Scholarship" as had Bruce McLaren before him. Raced Formula Junior on a shoestring, joined Brabham as mechanic in 1961. Raced Formula 2 Brabhams successfully, and finally joined Formula 1 Brabham team in 1966. World Champion 1967. Moved to McLaren 1968, stayed ever since, not likely to leave.

Ickx, Jacques Bernard (Jacky)—born Brussels, 1945, son of eminent Belgian motoring writer. Began competing with 50cc motorcycles, went to join Ken Tyrrell 1966 with Formula 2 Cooper after Belgian Army service. Immediate success; joined Ferrari 1968, first victory Rouen, in French Grand Prix. Went to Brabham in 1969, won two GPs. Returned to Ferrari for 1970 and became runner-up in World Championship. One of the three best drivers in the world.

McLaren, Bruce, 1937-1970—born Auckland, New Zealand, son of a garage owner and motorcyclist of repute. Learncd to drive in backyard, first hillclimb in 1952. Came to Europe under "Driver to Europe Scholarship" in 1958, went it alone for one year, then joined Cooper as Number 2 to Brabham. Won first GP in United States 1959. After Cooper, started his own business and began to build McLaren cars. Brilliant success in Can-Am; good in Formula 1. Finished third in Championship 1968, the year Hulme joined team. Killed testing 1970 Can-Am car at Goodwood, June 2, 1970.

Oliver, Jack—born Romford, England, 1942, son of refrigeration engineer. Started racing a Mini in 1960, joined Team Lotus for Formula 2 in 1967, moved up to Formula 1 team at Monaco 1968. Unlucky but useful year. Moved to BRM for 1969–71. Not won a Grand Prix yet, but far more success in sports cars.

Pescarolo, Henri—born Paris, France, 1942, son of a doctor. Raced Matra sports cars and Formula 2 and 1. Badly burned in practice for Le Mans 1968. Regular Number 2 driver in Matra Formula 1 during 1970.

Peterson, Ronnie—born Örebro, Sweden, 1944, son of a baker. Started to race karts and became Swedish champion, went on to drive a Formula 3 Brabham, and for Tecno in Formula 2. Now drives a March.

Regazzoni, Gian-Claudio (Clay)—born Lugano, Switzerland, 1939, son of a sheetmetal worker. Humble beginnings, carved his way through Formula 2 gaining an unenviable reputation for rough racing, but when put into Formula 1 Ferrari for occasional drives in 1970 calmed down, became a great professional, won the Austrian Grand Prix and finished the season as Ferrari's Number 2 to Ickx. A good possibility for champion's honors in 1971.

Rindt, Karl Jochen, 1942-1970—born in Mainz, Germany, son of a spice-mill owner, wealthy family. Parents killed in bombing raid 1943, Jochen brought up by grandparents in Graz, Austria. Always competitive in anything he did, from Ping-Pong to gin rummy. Jochen learned to ski and to drive early and very well. He also spoke near-perfect idiomatic English. First car Simca-Montléry, first competition, hillclimbs in Austria. Bought Alfa Romeo later, began to beat everybody in sight. Formula Junior 1963, bought Brabham F2 and won at Crystal Palace, astonishing everyone, 1964. Factory Cooper drive, then Brabham 1968. Joined Lotus 1969, rather disastrous year through mechanical failures. Shot ahead in 1970 with Lotus 72 and collected 45 Championship points by German GP. Killed in practice at Monza, September 1970. Second in ability possibly only to Stewart. World Champion 1970.

Rodriguez, Pedro—born Mexico City, 1940, elder son of one of the wealthiest men in Mexico. Brother Ricardo and he rode motorcycles at eleven, were racing at thirteen. Pedro went to college for two years while Ricardo took over beating everyone else in the game, and then they both went on to cars. The family had the money, the boys had the talent. Ricardo killed in practice for Mexican Grand Prix in 1962. Pedro has raced sports cars and Formula 1 machinery of almost every famous make, but always seemed underrated. Now with BRM, won Belgian GP in 1970—and almost the U.S.—he is a very strong, determined, likeable character. With the right car, could beat anyone.

Siffert, Joseph—born Fribourg, Switzerland, 1937, son of farm laborer. "Seppi" has had to come up the very hardest way—saving, and buying whatever machinery he could. Started with motorcycles, a 125 Gilera in 1957. He became Champion of Switzerland on a 350cc bike in 1959, and almost starved to do it. First car a Lotus 18 Formula Junior, then a Lotus 20 in 1961, all on his own money. Rob Walker Lotus 1965-69, won his first Grand Prix, the British, in 1968. Went to March as factory driver for 1970, now moving on to BRM. Has done *very* well in sports cars.

Stewart, Jackie—born Dunbartonshire, Scotland, 1939. Clay pigeon-shooting champion, and Olympic standard shot. Remarkable coordination of eye and hand. First car, green A35, then red

Jean-Pierre Beltoise

Ronnie Peterson   **François Cevert**

MG. Raced Marcos in Scottish events, then came farther afield with a Jaguar, under program name of A. N. Other to avoid upsetting his mother. Came to Ken Tyrrell's notice, very impressive debut in Formula 3. Went to BRM for Formula 1 in 1965, won first Grand Prix at Monza that year. Left BRM to join Ken Tyrrell in running Matra Fords at beginning of 1968, runner-up to Hill in Championship, took the title in 1969. Currently considered the world's Number One driver, certainly by me.

Surtees, John—born Surrey, 1934, son of motorcyclist mother and father. World-famous motorcycle champion, seven times! Four wheels in 1960 with Cooper, went to Ferrari in 1963, became World Champion in 1964. Two years with Honda, one with BRM, after quarrel with Ferrari. Began to build Surtees racing cars in 1969. John is an engineer, a designer, a tester, a competitor, an entrant, a team manager and anything else that comes his way. He survived one terrible accident in Canada in a sports car race, keeps his counsel and his loyal followers, and can always spring a surprise. The new Formula 1 Surtees Ford could be a very good car in 1971.

Stommelen, Rolf—born in Köln, Germany, 1943, son of garage owner. Began career in 1964, in a Porsche. Won Targa Florio in 1967 with Paul Hawkins, added Daytona and Paris 1000Ks. Now drives Formula 2 for Eifelland Caravans, of Mayen, and sports cars for Alfa Romeo. In 1970 was second driver to Jack Brabham on Brabham team, in his first season of Formula 1. A good prospect.

THE CARS

BEFORE THE DESIGN of racing cars became completely divorced from production cars, the prime object of winning a Grand Prix was to enhance the prestige of the victorious car, thus leading to a considerable increase in sales. Even if the racing cars were a bit in advance of those on the road, it was explained simply in the phrase "racing improves the breed." There is no doubt that this was a fact. Whether it remains true now is exceedingly debatable. The internal-combustion engine must be living out its last few years at the moment, and really justifiable claims of improving the breed can only be made by those who are already experimenting with other forms of propulsion.

Ever since 1906, those in charge of motor racing (the Automobile Club of France and later the FIA) have changed the regulations frequently, partly with the intention of making the sport safer; to slow the cars rather than make them faster. And every change has been thwarted by the designers of racing cars, the makers of tires, the geniuses behind each significant engine. Speeds constantly go up, even if the engine capacity goes down, for some-

28

Jackie Stewart gave car owner Ken Tyrrell his first victory as a car builder when he won the 1971 Spanish GP in his Tyrrell Ford.

one will find a way to improve roadholding or aerodynamics as a substitute for sheer brute strength.

Any book on motor racing is inevitably out of date before it leaves the typewriter, let alone the printer. Even now next year's Formula 1 cars are being designed and constructed in various parts of England, France, Italy and Germany. Next year's engines, or rather improvements on this year's, are occupying most of the thoughts and time of their designers, while others are pondering rotary piston engines and gas turbines. Changes are made all through the season, to combat changing circuit conditions or to iron out teething troubles on new cars. Every Grand Prix race report could run to book length if every minute modification were described, every experiment investigated.

If, therefore, I gloss over today's Grand Prix cars in a somewhat superficial way, it is only to avoid my words being of as much use to you in understanding Formula 1 racing as a description of a dodo.

The Lotus 72 is an extremely wedge-shaped car with the radiators at the sides instead of in front.

So, a typical Formula 1 car currently competing will have an engine of 8 or 12 cylinders developing between 420 and 460 bhp at over 10,000 rpm. It will be a mid-engined car (the engine is behind the driver and in front of the rear wheels) which is at the moment the best method of distributing the weight. Most cars have now progressed from the old tubular "space-frame" construction to the sheet metal "monocoque" design—which means that the body and chassis are built as one structure. The tires are enormously wide—up to 20 inches across at the rear—and regulation size "wings" are fitted to obtain the maximum possible downthrust.

The driver sits low and semi-reclining, surrounded by fuel contained in rubber-bag tanks which are foam-filled to reduce the fire risk following an impact such as happened at the Spanish Grand Prix in 1970. The regulations also require roll-over bars and fire extinguishers to cut down some of the inescapable risk. Commercial fuel—ordinary pump gasoline—has been used for some years as an improvement on the highly volatile mixtures which used to be employed. (Fuel, and its all-too-ready explosiveness, is still one of the greatest bones of contention within the sport, and is likely to continue being so until someone invents a non-inflammable substitute. If the space age can't produce one soon, we don't deserve to be so conceited about technological development.)

The manufacturers involved in Grand Prix racing are, at the time of writing, Ferrari, Lotus, Brabham, McLaren, BRM, March, Matra, Surtees and Tyrrell. Others may come forward in 1971, but at present there are only rumors. The engines employed are the Ferrari flat 12, the Matra Simca V12, the BRM V12, the Alfa Romeo V8 and the Ford V8. Until August 1970 the Cosworth-designed Ford DFV V8 had enjoyed an almost uninterrupted run of success since 1967, winning thirty-three out of forty-one races. Then the Ferrari, after some years of great potential and a bad reliability record, fulfilled its promise and won three of the last four races of the 1970 season.

However, the new Tyrrell Ford, designed by Derek Gardner and driven by Jackie Stewart, left the Ferraris standing for the first

The complexity of the rear end of the Lotus 72 is readily apparent in this photo, which shows the suspension, battery, oil tank, inboard brakes and engine.

The 312B is the newest Ferrari to compete for the championship.

laps of the Canadian Grand Prix and showed up even better at Watkins Glen. It led Ickx's Ferrari by thirty seconds after fifty-two laps of the 108 lap race before an oil pipe chafed through, and there is no reason why the Tyrrell/Ferrari battle should not be a very brisk one in 1971. Lotus may come up with an even better 72, or they may be allowed to run their gas-turbine car, unless regulations are hastily changed.

But all this is speculation. As the 1970 season has just ended, it is of 1970 cars only that I can write. Let's start with the World Champion, Lotus.

Lotus, which is now a group of companies making both racing and road cars, is based at Hethel, in Norfolk, England. It was in the airplane hanger at Hethel that the Lotus 72 was unveiled on April 6, 1970, with a great blast of publicity. After three years of the very successful Lotus 49, Colin Chapman had reverted to the wedge shape which was the significant feature of his 1968 Indianapolis car. There were a number of other innovations, notably inboard front brakes and variable rate springing. Its greatest asset was probably its excellent penetration and low unsprung weight.

The 72 was intended to be a world-beater built for a World Champion. Lotus did, in fact, win the Constructors' Championship for the fourth time and Jochen Rindt became World Champion after scoring five victories. However, because two of these were the result of Jack Brabham's bad luck, and because Rindt was killed in practice for the Italian Grand Prix (a race which might have shown once and for all whether or not the Lotus 72 was all Colin Chapman had hoped), the year ended on an inconclusive note. I say this reluctantly, and not in a denigrating way at all. But I know that Colin Chapman would have preferred those five victories to have been from flag to flag, and preferably in straight, evenly matched competition with Stewart, the only driver he considered Rindt's rival. In addition, the only time the Lotus *beat* the Ferrari with both still in contention at the end was at Hockenheim, in the German Grand Prix. That was definitely the 72's—and Jochen's—finest victory. The best of all contests is one we shall now never see: Jochen Rindt in the 72 versus Jackie Stewart in the Tyrrell.

The Ferrari, runner-up in both constructors' and drivers' championships (Jacky Ickx ended the year only five points behind Jochen's total of forty-five) somehow took on a new lease of life in 1970. It is a very beautiful car, with a typical Ferrari chassis of

The Ferrari flat 12 engine is hung from this rearward extension of the chassis which consists of small diameter tubes and stressed skin.

The Ferrari flat 12 engine.

small diameter tubes to which sheet aluminum is riveted, with an extended rear section from which the flat 12 engine is hung. This engine, which was being tested during the latter months of 1969, improved steadily throughout the year, and there were several different versions of it to suit individual circuits—different bore and stroke ratios, valve sizes and valve angles—which made it a potential winner anywhere in the world.

It was unfortunate, to say the least, that in the second of the season's thirteen Grands Prix, the Spanish, Ickx's Ferrari should have been rammed amidships by Jackie Oliver's BRM on the first lap. The resulting holocaust destroyed both cars, and the burns Ickx suffered took a very long time to heal. This prevented his being competitive until the Dutch GP where he finished third, and from then on he never looked back.

The arrival of the March into the world of motor racing was quite a phenomenon. The firm came into existence at the end of 1969, and with a team of very young men headed by ex-McLaren designer Robin Herd, they made a lot of promises and surprised everyone by keeping them. The first Formula 1 March was ready,

There were a lot of jokes about the "Instant Grand Prix Car" but, in fact, the March 701 came very near to being an instant success.

Jack Brabham is one of only three men to have won a Grand Prix in a car of his own design and manufacture and the only man to have become World Champion in his own car.

Above: Cockpit photo of the Brabham shows hex wrench taped to the wheel. In the event of a crash the steering wheel can be removed to facilitate getting the driver out without waiting for a mechanic to arrive.

As with many current cars in Formula racing, the Brabham chassis ends immediately behind the driver with the engine carrying the rear suspension.

The BRM V12 engine has four valves per cylinder.

The BRM 153 featured a twin-pontoon monocoque chassis.

Below: The 1970 BRM was a much improved car, and it was only bad luck that Pedro Rodriguez won but a single race.

as stated, on January 31, 1970; on a freezing day, the bright red car was finally pushed out of its shed as the light began to fade, and inside feverish activity was going on to ensure that there would be two cars for the Tyrrell team, two for the factory and one for Mario Andretti and the STP Corporation, before competition motoring began in South Africa on March 7—an appropriate date.

Subsequently, several more March Formula 1 cars were made and sold, and the firm's program included Formula 2, 3 and Can-Am machines as well. There were a lot of jokes about the "Instant Grand Prix Car," but, in fact, the March 701 came very near to being an "Instant Success"—no mean feat in such a competitive world. The factory drivers were Chris Amon and Jo Siffert, while Jackie Stewart and François Cevert (Johnny Servoz-Gavin for the first three Grands Prix) drove the new car for Ken Tyrrell. Apart from the STP Oil Treatment Special for Andretti, Ronnie Peterson ran one with great skill for Antique Automobiles.

There is no denying the March 701 was a strange car, which has improved and will improve still further. François Cevert described it as "like trying to drive two cars, one at the back and one at the front," while Stewart opted for the new Tyrrell as soon as it was raceworthy—in Canada. But in spite of its odd handling characteristics it had a remarkably successful year for an entirely new marque. Stewart and Amon set joint-fastest practice time at Kyalami, and Stewart finished third. Stewart won the Spanish Grand

The Matra was designed with the help of a number of brilliant engineers and designers from the French spacecraft and missile industry.

The Matra V12 engine seems to have a little less power than its competitors and has yet to win a race.

Prix and the Race of Champions, while Chris Amon won the Silverstone International Trophy Race, his first-ever Formula 1 victory. After this both Stewart and Amon gained good second places, but as the Lotus 72 and the Ferrari and the BRM improved, March found it harder to stay up in the top six.

The Brabham BT33, Ron Tauranac's first Formula 1 monocoque, started the year looking like a world-beater by winning in South Africa. The combination of the car, the Goodyear tires and Jack Brabham's unaltered skill and verve should have given them more victories. Subsequently two were snatched from Jack on the last lap and the Spanish was lost through a faulty crankshaft. At Monaco he was only yards from the finish when he made a wrong decision regarding a slower car in front of him at the gasworks hairpin, took it on the wrong side leaving his braking a fraction late and nudged gently into the strawbales. This let Jochen Rindt by to win, because Rindt had pulled up from thirteen seconds behind to one and a half seconds in the course of the last eleven laps—an astonishing feat.

In the British Grand Prix Jack had passed Jochen and pulled out a big lead which was totally irreversible, then ran out of fuel when in sight of the checkered flag on the last lap.

After that he seemed to have nothing but bad luck of all kinds, and finished his long and illustrious racing career in Mexico with a blown engine while lying a comfortable third. He has now retired

The McLaren is a conventional car which won no races in 1970, but with which Denis Hulme finished in the top four in half of the year's races.

from Grand Prix racing but the Brabham cars will go on, and Jack himself will be involved with Indianapolis and possibly other forms of American racing. The Brabham car first entered competition motoring in 1962, and under the company name of Motor Racing Developments, designer Ron Tauranac has built sound and reliable cars, which twice won the Constructors' Championship—1966 and 1967. There is still a lot of potential in Motor Racing Developments and they can never be underestimated.

The BRM has a very long and varied history, mostly of much-publicized failure. There is already more than one book on the subject. But in 1970 the car was better than I have ever known it in my thirteen years of Grand Prix racing, and it has an entirely new look in almost every way. The P153, using a much revised version of the 48-valve BRM V12 engine, had a low, wide monocoque chassis with a tubular subframe under the engine. For the first time BRM accepted outside sponsorship, and was decked out very smartly in the colors of Yardley, the cosmetic firm, which must have spent an enormous amount of money during the year on this "production." Unfortunately, the BRM had only one victory, Pedro Rodriguez winning convincingly at Spa. He very nearly

Above: A semi-circular steering wheel on Hulme's McLaren makes getting in and out of the tight-fitting cockpit a little easier.

Left: The McLaren cockpit with oil pipes, brake lines and throttle cable passing under the seat.

While the factory McLarens are powered by Ford engines, this one, driven by Andrea de Adamich, has an Alfa Romeo.

repeated the performance at Watkins Glen, but ran out of fuel eight laps from the flag and was passed by Emerson Fittipaldi in his Lotus 72. Both Pedro and Jackie Oliver collected Championship points during the year, Pedro finishing seventh in the table, but he was unlucky not to be higher.

The French Matra team, like BRM and Ferrari, makes its own engine as well as the chassis, whereas the rest of the current Formula 1 cars use the Ford V8 engine and an almost identical list of components. While Ferrari has Fiat backing, Matra has government and Chrysler (Simca) money to bolster it up. Because they are an offshoot of the spacecraft and missile industry of France, they have any number of brilliant engineers and designers to call upon, most with an aeronautical background. Looking at the Matra, and seeing its many and varied problems, I can't help thinking that the whole thing needs simplifying drastically. The car has always incorporated some very advanced engineering, and as I am no engineer it is impertinent for me to comment in this way. But although the Matra chassis took Jackie Stewart to the world championship crown in 1969, using the Ford V8 engine, the Matra in its all-French form with the V12 engine has never won a race. It should. But the engine seems to be down on power by comparison with the Ford and the other 12-cylinder cars. The team doesn't seem happy with their tires, and they have all manner of engine and fuel-feed troubles. I don't know the answer, but maybe Matra will suddenly emerge in 1971 as the unbeatable "missile" it should be, and Vive la France!

The McLaren is a conventional car, a very good second or third runner in the hands of former Champion Denny Hulme, but not a winner in 1970. They had terrible problems, with Denny's burnt hands and the death of Bruce McLaren himself, but even taking these facts into account, the McLaren—which after all uses the same Ford V8 engine as almost everyone else—will have to be just a bit faster to cope with the Tyrrell and the Ferrari in the future. In Can-Am they are unbeatable, but as Bruce himself said not long before he died, "in Formula 1 we are just scratching to keep up,"

**John Surtees has joined the still select list of drivers who have built
and competed in their own cars.**

and he intended to do something about that. Whether it can be done
without him remains to be seen.

Another new car of interest emerged in 1970—John Surtees at
last turned constructor and produced a handsome, fast and competitive car, the Surtees TS7. It handles very well, uses the Ford
engine, and John has obviously picked up pointers along the way
by driving for Ferrari and Honda. With his star-studded years of
experience behind him, what John needs now is a bit of luck to put
his Surtces up at the front of the grid.

That, then, is a very brief look at the 1970 Formula 1 cars,
totally ignoring the de Tomaso and the Bellasi. On the shop floor
at nearby Byfleet there is already a prototype Brabham BT34,
March has its 1971 car virtually ready for inspection, and all the
other factories, if they are to be in with a chance at Kyalami,
South Africa, on March 6, will have new cars in much the same
stages of readiness. By the time you read this they will be racing.

THE CONSTRUCTORS
AND DESIGNERS

GRAND PRIX CARS are conceived, designed and built by small groups of people, usually working together closely in very unglamorous surroundings. They all have one aim in mind—to produce a Formula 1 car that will go faster than the others, and stay in one piece. During the present formula, which began in 1966, we have seen designers run through a great number of innovations within the limits of the FIA rules—and sometimes a little outside them! We have had the era of suspension-mounted "wings" and experiments with four-wheel-drive, while gas turbine and/or rotary engines have been toyed with, at least on the drawing board if not on the circuit.

A Grand Prix car can be the brain-child of one man, but it will usually be drawn by someone else, built by a few very skilled mechanics and modified or changed in detail as the season progresses. It is sometimes difficult to know where to apportion praise or blame for the design of a car, and even within a team the originator of the basic idea will blame the designer-draftsman when things go

Enzo Ferrari   **Colin Chapman**

wrong, and vice versa, while both will blame the mechanics whenever possible!

It is not feasible to talk in the abstract on this subject, because each make of Grand Prix car comes into being in a different way. Different nationalities are involved, different philosophies, different methods of bringing a car to life, although the end products bear a remarkable similarity.

Colin Chapman and Lotus are synonymous. The Lotus Grand Prix car, the first of which appeared at the start of the 1958 season, is the product of Chapman's early years as a "specials" builder and sports car designer. Colin is a civil engineering graduate of London University, and built his first car on an old Austin 7 chassis while he was still a student. The bodywork was of plywood, the whole thing was put together in a rented garage in the evenings, and when ready was entered for trials—two, to be exact, in both of which he scored class wins. Examinations intervened, but the next year, 1949, he went on to build another Lotus. This time he installed a Ford 10 engine in an Austin 7 chassis and went racing. He could have been a racing driver, more than likely of

Ron Tauranac   **Mauro Forghieri**

world championship class, but his urge to design and build overcame his pursuit of race driving as a profession.

The Mark 6 was the first real Lotus as it was based on a new chassis designed by Chapman and was the forerunner of all he has built since—inventive, different, lightweight, successful. After service in the Royal Air Force and a spell as a project engineer with British Aluminium, Colin was virtually forced into business as a manufacturer by the tremendous demand for replicas of the Lotus 6. Since then, all the way along the line, the success of his products has demanded growth at a rate and of a magnitude that Colin himself never really intended or envisaged. Sometimes it has scared him, but mostly he has looked at the challenge, found it tempting and not only accepted it but delighted in it. His attitude toward his "empire" is contradictory—on one side he resents its intrusion into his deepest involvement, Grand Prix racing, and on the other he has enjoyed becoming a millionaire.

Colin Chapman has received most of the rewards available to a manufacturer, and most of the abuse (mixed with admiration) which successful men usually encounter. He began life with a very efficient brain, plus the little extra that people tend to call genius. He has been hard-working and astute, charming enough to command intense loyalty and ruthless enough to use and cast aside a number of people on his way to the top. He is The Boss; no matter how much work he delegates to others, the only person who ever *really* gets things moving is Colin, whether it is the running of a new Formula 1 car, or the installing of a typists' lavatory, or the smoothing-down of ruffled shareholders.

These days the designs on his drawing table at home are mostly of light airplanes, but he is still and will always be, I think, the brain behind each new Lotus. There is a vast staff at the Lotus factory in Norfolk, not the least of whom are the designers and draftsmen. Maurice Phillipe, his Chief Designer, acts perhaps more as a rein on Colin's runaway ideas than a designer in his own right. But between them they manage to come up with "the car to beat" almost every year.

There have been triumphs and catastrophes, magnificent victories and ignominious defeats. Bruce McLaren once said that, "Chapman innovates for the sake of innovating," and sometimes it works and sometimes it doesn't. But Colin is the man in motor racing to whom most people look for a lead, even if they don't want to. He has been accused of "cheating" the FIA regulations many times; his cars have been impounded more than once for close scrutiny after an accident. Lotus has been World Champion Constructor four times in less than a decade. Either you love them or you hate them—Lotus and Chapman; they are one and the same.

Ferrari, maybe, comes nearest to Lotus in the intensity of its competition and the dominance of the man at the top. Although Enzo Ferrari is now subsidized by Fiat money and is no longer seen at Grands Prix other than the Italian, he is still the greatest autocrat in motor racing, one of those living legends we hear about. He began his career as a racing driver for Alfa Romeo, in the twenties one of the biggest names in the business, though with men like Nuvolari and Varzi on the racing team, Ferrari was not the most famous driver of his time.

His whole life, apart from the fact that he never graduated as a qualified engineer, runs remarkably parallel to Colin Chapman's. He has always had this quality of leadership, the ability to inspire people and to collect about him other great talents. Scuderia Ferrari began when Alfa Romeo officially withdrew from racing in the late twenties, and Enzo returned to Modena to open his own modest work shops where he prepared Alfas for racing. In the thirties marriage, fatherhood and finally the Second World War put an end to his own motor racing.

During the war he worked with a firm in Rome making small four-cylinder engines for training aircraft, and later set up his own factory to build machines for the manufacture of ball bearings. After the war he moved his business to Maranello near Modena, and at last some of the many ideas on the making of racing cars that had been forming in his head throughout the years could be allowed to bear fruit.

Where Chapman's design philosophy rests on low weight, excellent roadholding and good aerodynamics, Ferrari's is mostly based on power, plus the best drivers in the world. The fact that his cars are also very beautiful to look at is very much an Italian trait. A Ferrari car uses a Ferrari engine; nearly all its parts are made by Ferrari or subcontracted to firms who work *for* Ferrari almost exclusively. Men working at Maranello now are working alongside their fathers, and maybe their sons too. It is that sort of society. As Ferrari himself has said, he employs young men fresh from technical schools and colleges, and men from the old days of Scuderia Ferrari, thus bringing together impulsive and energetic recruits and those who stand for the tradition of quality and loyalty. It seems to pay off. Ferrari, since the first car of its name raced at Piacenza in 1947 (a 12-cylinder $1\frac{1}{2}$-liter car, otherwise fairly orthodox), has had the best success record of *any* racing car manufacturer.

Toward the end of 1969 I was asked by Ford of England to

Derek Gardner   **Robin Herd**

count up the number of *consecutive* wins by any one engine; they
rather hoped to find they had beaten all records with the Cosworth
V8. Well, I counted. Ferrari won, 14 to 11. But that wasn't all.
The startling thing, looking down the old tables of Grand Prix
results, was that from 1950 to 1958 Ferrari had won no less than
twenty-seven Grands Prix, and taken the first three places in several events. 1959 and 1960 were Cooper years, but Ferrari was
back with a winner in 1961, carrying off the championship both
then and in 1964.

Since then, victories have been sparse, but the combination of
the flat 12 engine and the talents of Ickx, Regazzoni and Giunti
almost made it in 1970. Power and drivers—the old formula for
Ferrari success. Add the brilliant engineering ability and mature
mind of Mauro Forghieri, and 1971 should be a vintage year for
the marque.

Forghieri has worked for Ferrari since leaving Bologna University with a Doctorate in engineering, but was more of an engine

specialist than a chassis man when given the task of taking over control of the racing division from Carlo Chiti at the age of twenty-six. He was thrown in at the deep end, and there have been many who wanted to prevent the young engineer from following his own ideas. At last it seems that Mauro has come out of the ups and downs of Ferrari fortunes as the new leader, his ideas vindicated. He attends every Grand Prix, in the manner of Colin Chapman, and is, for the first time, really "in charge." It seems to be paying off.

The Brabham—or the Tauranac, depending upon how you view things—has won the constructors' championship twice in the present formula, 1966 and 1967. The cars are made by Motor Racing Developments, a company formed by Jack Brabham and Ron Tauranac in 1961. Jack had long wanted to build his own cars, as he had built his own midget racers for speedway driving back in Australia, and after winning the World Drivers' Championship twice (1959 and 1960), he was financially ready and experienced enough to try out some of his ideas of what a racing car should be. He had worked with Ron Tauranac back in Sydney, they had even raced against each other at one stage, and when it came to design, Jack knew Ron was the man to have on the team.

Jack himself is a great driver and a great practical mechanic. But he says, "I left all the designing to Ron. He had all the technical background, whereas mine was only practical. We worked together and we understood one another—we were complementary to one another. I got him to come over here in 1961, and even then I never tried to do the technical drawing side. When I drove the car we used to talk about it technically and got together on improving it."

Perhaps one of the most remarkable things about MRD is that their cars are "right" as soon as they reach a track. They may have to make slight modifications during practice, but they do not go testing in the way most other teams do. Ron reckons to design and build a car that is ready to race at the beginning of the season, and admits to being more interested in detail work than in the overall

50

concept of the car. He knows he can build a good chassis, the Ford V8 engine is a known quantity, and it is therefore the changes needed to accommodate the growth of tire width and the improvement of roadholding by downthrust devices that send Ron back to the drawing board.

The car was never intended to be called a Brabham, although the use of Jack's name must have meant greater interest initially. It was meant to be an MRD, as had the Formula Junior cars which the firm first built. Only the unfortunate sound the initials made when spoken by the French brought about the change to "Brabham!" And, of course, it stuck. The designation of each design as a BT simply stands for Brabham and Tauranac. Now that Jack has retired from motor racing Ron will go on making cars and running the Grand Prix team. The BT34, Ron tells me, is as different from the 33 as the Lotus 72 was from the 49, and, providing he can find a top driver for the team, there is no reason why his cars should be any less competitive in the future than over the past five years.

Robin Herd came from the aircraft industry, via McLaren and Cosworth, to design the March. He is a clever, handsome, plausible young man who gained a double first at Oxford University, and from his undergraduate days was always interested in making a racing car to his own ideas. Some of these he tried at McLaren, where, under Bruce's direction, he worked on most of the early Formula 1 and Can-Am designs. Others were incorporated in the four-wheel-drive Cosworth. This car was never raced, though it put up some very promising performances during tests.

Herd designed the first Formula 1 March to a set of very simple basic principles; but this was necessary if the newly formed firm was to get the promised quota of cars ready to race by the South African Grand Prix in March. There was nothing very novel about the March 701, but it made a fairly good showing throughout the year, and the 711, the 1971 March, will undoubtedly incorporate some more sophisticated thinking.

In 1969 BRM designer Tony Southgate started work on a brand

new Formula 1 car for 1970. The P153 is a totally new conception for a BRM, using their own 12-cylinder engine in a wide, low, rather bulbous bodyshape, everything designed for quick engine changes, which were difficult before.

Southgate came to BRM from Lola and AAR, and according to BRM's record, seems to have done their rather stuffy image some good. Until Pedro Rodriguez won at Spa this year, BRM hadn't had a Grand Prix victory since Jackie Stewart won at Monaco in 1966. Even now, with a much better chassis and some of the early bugs removed from the design, they still need engine-reliability. But Tony's work has stirred up a few of the implacable BRM critics to take another look at the marque, and Yardley has not withdrawn its sponsorship—which they would certainly do if there were no promise of success for 1971.

Derek Gardner evidently had a good look at the Matra MS80 before designing the Tyrrell Ford. This latter car proved at the Canadian and U.S. Grands Prix that Derek was on the right road. Things went wrong, but when Jackie Stewart built up a 30-second lead at Watkins Glen people began to sit up and take notice. Derek Gardner was appropriated by Ken Tyrrell from Harry Ferguson Research early in 1970, and the Tyrrell was built in the most complete secrecy I have ever known in motor racing. Derek is a diffident, thoughtful man, who lay awake all night in Canada worrying over his design, and whether he could advise Ken Tyrrell to take a chance on using the car for a vital round in the championship or stick to the well-tried but badly handling March. (Tyrrell has never pretended to be a designer—he is a great manager, talent spotter and organizer, but not an engineer.) Jackie Stewart has a lot of faith in the car, and once he and Derek between them have solved all the problems which beset most new Grand Prix cars, I envisage another great year for the Tyrrell/Stewart combination.

Of the rest of the Formula 1 constructors, Surtees seems to have the best potential. He has designed, drawing on his past experience with Coopers, Lotuses, Ferraris, Hondas, and BRMs, a very clean-lined, straightforward, Ford-engined car, the TS7. John is a per-

52

Keith Duckworth   **Ken Tyrrell**

fectionist, and has been accused of an almost paranoic insistence on perfection in others. He has never been truly happy as someone else's driver, and always wanted to create something of his own. It is this desire to create something which most of the people who had to deal with him as a team member in the past did not understand. Perhaps John didn't either. But with his own factory and his own name on a Grand Prix car, John Surtees smiles a great deal more than he has done for many years. He is a bit of an artist, in fact, and a very ambitious one.

The Matra chassis designer is Bernard Boyer, and his work is highly respected throughout the industry. The car has always been renowned for its good roadholding and handling. Matra Simca has a great deal of money, a vast reserve of talent to call upon and the most advanced racing development premises and equipment anywhere. But the all-French Matra Formula 1 car has never won a Grand Prix. They need to solve their two main problems of fuel starvation and breaking valve springs—and they also need to be a lot less secretive about the car and what they do down there at Velizy, France. (Trying to get near the Matra factory is rather like trying to get into the control room at Houston or the launching area at Cape Kennedy.)

McLarens I shall not dwell upon. Since Bruce's untimely death, the impetus seems to have gone out of the Formula 1 side of the organization. Bruce had his own very definite ideas about producing racing cars, of which I shall quote one or two; but who else can take his place? Will they care enough about Formula 1 to go on making Grand Prix cars at all?

"First of all," Bruce used to say, "in motor racing you are designing to a time deadline. What you have to do is come up with a car that is slightly better than someone else's but you've got to do it *now*. There's no way you can design a car ten years in the future. But you can design next year's car and get it *running*—that's the philosophy around here anyway. And strong and efficient is better than delicate and beautiful as far as I am concerned. But we'll probably never reach our ideal car because we are learning all the time."

That is the whole point, really. A constructor or designer is feeling his way, sometimes amid the minute detail, sometimes in the overall conception, toward an ideal. And as soon as he thinks he may have reached it someone else has come up with a better idea, and he wonders why he hadn't thought of it himself. Keith Duckworth, designer of the fabulous Cosworth V8 engine, once said, "Development is only necessary because of the ignorance of designers." Now there's a provocative statement—it leaves you plenty to argue about.

THE MECHANICS,
THEIR LIFE AND WORK

"*BEING AN ORDINARY* garage mechanic is just about the end of the world. Most race mechanics are those who have discovered this and are trying to get away from a mundane type of existence. Garage work is all right for a young boy, an apprentice, but there is no way anyone with a spark of adventure can do that job all his life."

That is the opinion of one who knows. Mike Barney began adult life as a garage apprentice, went to Cooper in its best days as Bruce McLaren's mechanic, moved on to McLaren as chief mechanic when Bruce left Cooper, and is now a Prototype Builder at Motor Racing Developments (Brabham).

"If you are interested in cars at all, then the ultimate must be a racing car, and you go from bread-and-butter work on somebody's old Ford, or what have you, and try to get a job with a racing team. There is a lot more adventure involved in racing cars, right from the building of them to the racing of them. Almost all the mechanics I know have worked in a garage before coming into racing, but

they have to be rather special people to *stay* in racing, because it has some very harsh aspects."

Jack Brabham says that a racing car is only as good as the preparation that goes into it—and he should know. He started his career as a garage hand, became a skilled mechanic, learning how to make almost anything required to keep a car running when spare parts were virtually impossible to obtain during and after the war, and went on to put all his practical experience into the cars that bear his name.

There is no doubt that a man has to be deeply interested in the way a mechanic works to start with, and this is something, a gift like any other I suppose, with which you are born. The two-year-old boy who is keen only on toys which he can take to pieces and is content to make endless permutations of constructions using wooden bricks, has the makings of a mechanic or maybe an engineer. His later schooling will decide which direction his career will take, but the difference is not necessarily one of intelligence—it is a different approach to the same problems. In motor racing, the engineer or designer wants his car to be the best, the winner, the world-beater. The mechanic, while he would prefer his car to win,

56

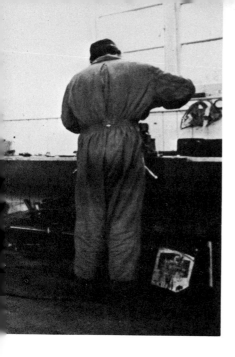

The mechanic's life consists mainly of many long hours of hard work.

primarily wants it to stay together, thus proving that the job of preparation was thoroughly done.

The old folk rhyme, "For the want of a nail . . ." could be applied to motor racing with great aptness. Many's the race that has been lost through the failure of some small component, which may never have given any trouble before even in hundreds of miles of testing. But sometimes—very rarely—it is known that the failure was due to negligence by a mechanic, and this can be a difficult burden to bear, especially if a driver has been hurt as a result. This human error element is almost impossible to rule out, particularly when a team of mechanics may have gone without sleep or proper food for perhaps thirty-six or more hours. It is up to the chief mechanic to try to organize things so that, in theory, negligence is not a word in the mechanic's vocabulary—but even *his* efforts are sometimes thwarted by an ambitious team manager or constructor.

To become the chief mechanic on a racing team, particularly in Formula 1, you have to be sharper and quicker than the others, as well as have that indefinable quality of leadership. Usually, the chief mechanic has come "from the ranks" and now has to tell his

57

former mates what to do. This calls for a certain temperament—apart from having proved himself better at the job than they are, he has to command respect without being rude or in any way unpleasant, and see that every man in his team pulls his weight. He is often the whipping boy for the team manager *and* the target of murmured abuse from his juniors—no enviable position.

The practice of having certain mechanics, usually two, to look after one driver's car instead of the whole team pitching in and trying to cope with two or three cars simultaneously, has proved to be a good measure which has grown up in recent years. The car's success becomes a matter of personal pride, and there seems a greater involvement between mechanic, driver and race than there used to be.

This scheme is fine provided circumstances are favorable. If, for instance, one of the team's cars has been involved in a shunt during the final practice session, then all the boys will rally round to get the car to the starting line at all cost. What could normally be termed miracles have been performed in this way, sometimes with rewarding results, sometimes with heartbreaking disappointment. I remember Jim Endruweit, for several years chief mechanic for the Lotus Formula 1 team, telling me of a night spent in a damp concrete garage, "somewhere in Europe," rain streaming down outside (and sometimes in) while he and his colleagues changed the engine and straightened the bodywork of a car that had been more than a little "modified" late in the afternoon of the day before the race. The mechanics had no sleep for almost forty-eight hours, survived mainly on Coca-Cola and sandwiches, got the car to the line on time, only to see it fall by the wayside within a few laps of the finish line, while leading. All that is left then is to pack up the transporter and go home and, like the driver, wait till the next race.

One of the worst problems of being a Formula 1 mechanic is that of getting enough sleep. With thirteen Grands Prix on the calendar, most only two weeks apart, and several other Formula 1 races, there isn't much time to drive the transporter back to base, strip the cars down (or make new ones), load up and be at the next venue in good time. And as there are only twenty-four hours in a day, quite a few of the night ones get eaten up with traveling, plus overnight engine, suspension or gear ratio changes after the first day of practice.

Mike Barney's personal maximum was two days and two nights without closing an eye.

"Whereupon we finished in a ditch! Transporter, cars and all. The time to stop is when you are getting well into your second wind—after the dreadful drowsiness, the dizzy feeling, the light-headed hours. You go through these and come out the other side, and you think you can go on indefinitely. You get to know that that feeling doesn't last long. After that it becomes psychological. If you can keep your mind active and keep busy you're all right, but the minute you relax—wham! You're asleep.

"I've seen a lot of people come and go because they couldn't stand the pace—not specifically because they couldn't stay awake

The paddock where the mechanics work on their cars at Clermont-Ferrand can perhaps best be described as rustic.

Race tire fitting can require
a great deal of exertion.

all night, but being away from home so much, not traveling well, girl friends or wives getting niggly, all sorts of reasons. And if there are children as well, it's difficult for a man to be away from home so much, leaving his wife to cope with all the disasters and the sheer loneliness of being the only parent.

"That American trip—from Canada, through Watkins Glen to Mexico—it's a great trip to go on, but you're away from home about seven weeks. It is an education in itself, but by the time you reach Mexico—! Well, you've done Watkins Glen, you've been to the bowling alley, you've seen New York, you've had ten days in the cheaper parts of Acapulco, and then you arrive in Mexico City, no money left, for the annual fight with the Mexicans. At your hotel they've lost your booking, they've never heard of you, even if you booked three months in advance. 'Try so-and-so, just ten blocks away.' So you try that one, they don't know anything about it, don't even know what day it is. You go around to all the seedier hotels in Mexico City till you arrive back at the one you booked into, and surprise, surprise, they've found the letter! Ah, you're Senor X!' 'Well, I told you that in the first place.' And so it goes on. The shower doesn't work, the toilet doesn't work, the lights fall apart . . . by the time the race is over, you're so sick of your team-mates—because you've been with them for the last six or seven weeks, living out of the same grotty suitcases, all your clothes stink, everything stinks—you just want to go home, and hibernate for about six months."

Not that you'll ever see any real friction between mechanics. Everything simply goes all quiet when they are under stress. They stop whistling and making jokes, and only after the race, when a few beers have loosened their tongues and relaxed them again, will their normal, extraordinarily cheerful and nonchalant demeanor return.

Each mechanic on the team has his own job to do and must see that it gets done.

The interior of the McLaren factory where the cars are meticulously prepared for racing.

There is another major problem in the world of the mechanic, which is, in a nutshell, that you can never plan things down to the last detail, check the job list, tighten every nut and bolt and know nothing will break—because something most likely will. There are a lot of unknown factors in the behavior of a racing car. Even if the design, the engineering, the building and preparation of a car are of the highest quality, no one can cater for the infinite possibilities of stress—the number of times the car hits a curb at Monaco, comes off the ground at the Nürburgring or bottoms at Brands Hatch. How do you calculate just how much punishment a car and its components are going to take in the course of a race meeting? There is no way.

(If everything were made stronger, a car would never fall to pieces but it would be so heavy it would drive like a bus and be far too slow. In fact, not a racing car at all.)

Vibration is another incalculable cause of breakages of one sort or another. A worn part somewhere deep in the engine, for instance, can set up a vibration during a race, and shatter all sorts

of things that have never broken before. Vibrations in the gear
train can knock the teeth off gears in the transmission; even the
motor itself can destroy its own timing gears. At certain speeds,
in certain places, on certain tracks, some very minor part that has
grown a little tired can cause absolute havoc without any previous
warning. And some problems are never satisfactorily solved at all.

So job lists are very nice, and check and double check most desirable, but bad luck can crop up and ruin all a mechanic's careful
work—and his work is invariably careful, otherwise he would
never have reached the stage of looking after a Formula 1 car.
One ideal attempt at a solution would be to have someone to go
around each car before a race and, maybe after two or three mechanics have spent all night stripping a car down to the chassis,
welding, putting it all back together again with about half an hour
to spare before the race, check absolutely everything possible. He'd
have to be fresh, wide awake and competent, which means employ-
ing a spare, experienced mechanic especially for this purpose.
That idea has not yet been put into practice as far as I know. And

A mechanic's work is never done, for everything must be checked and
double checked and then checked again.

even then, bad luck might strike in yet another new place!

The *good* side of the racing mechanic's life is an opportunity to travel that only the armed forces could otherwise give him. He is doing a job he basically enjoys deeply, being not too badly paid for it by European standards, between $60 and $100 a week, and getting around from South Africa to Mexico via most countries in Europe and the States, all expenses paid. A mechanic could get exactly the same wages, maybe more, just around the corner at Joe Bloggs's Garage, but there is no adventure in that. And if he is at all keen on racing, the Grand Prix itself is a bonus every time, whether his team wins or not. Motor racing is full of disappointment, but it also has its high spots which are higher than almost anything else I know.

These few comments on the pros and cons of being a motor racing mechanic have to be generalizations. Each team has its own way of doing things, its own standards, its own priorities. Each team has a different man at the top, widely differing personalities. At Lotus, Colin Chapman is the man you have to answer to for mistakes, the one who bawls you out, the one who hugs you when Lotus has won a Grand Prix. Gordon Huckle is chief mechanic, and a very good one, while Dick Scammell is officially team manager. But when Colin is around, everyone knows who's boss!

Mauro Forghieri is Ferrari's top engineer, but he, too, is very much in charge at race meetings. Apart from a few regulars, Ferrari has always worked on a system by which Formula 1 mechanics are changed every few meetings. But during the latter half of this year I have seen the same faces appearing time and again. Perhaps that has something to do with the phenomenal success recently —continuity.

McLaren's personnel used to be the happiest bunch around the circuits. Sometimes they are still, but since Bruce's death, some of the familiar faces departed, a lot of the fun and games went out of the team, and they are like a small army without a leader. Alastair Caldwell is Formula 1 chief mechanic, a New Zealander like Bruce and Denny. Alastair is articulate, demanding, abrupt and stands

65

no nonsense even from his Number 1 driver. In Europe, McLaren Director Phil Kerr is often in charge overall, in the States either Teddy Mayer or Tyler Alexander. They are all very definite characters, really top men. But without Bruce they seem to have lost the spark that united them so closely.

The Brabham mechanics, having followed Jack through thick and thin, are now wondering whether it will all be worthwhile without him. There may be an almost entirely new team next year, sadly. Their chief mechanic, Ron Denis, has the makings of a constructor, I think.

BRM is in the care of Alan Challis, otherwise known as "Dobbin," who has been with the team quite a few years and worked his way to the top. They had reached a stage where most of the mechanics were much older than those in other teams, but the new life that Yardley promotion has put into BRM seems to have given everything a face-lift, and the team as a whole is running the better for it.

March mechanics were culled at the beginning of 1970 from all the other existing teams—one saw faces at the Bicester factory

The good side of the racing mechanic's life is the opportunity to travel. Here Goodyear tire fitters work alongside the swimming pool at Monaco.

A crew member signals Brabham that he has a lead of seven seconds, has lapped in one minute twenty-six and three-tenths seconds (the minute is left off) and that there are twelve laps to go.

which one had come to associate with Lotus, McLaren, Brabham, Indianapolis and Formula 2 racing. They "jelled" during the year into a comprehensible pattern, but it takes time for a team to become a distinct unit. Two of their best people went off with Mario Andretti to the United States, and who could blame them? The rewards of racing in America are far greater than in Europe.

Ken Tyrrell and Rob Walker have mechanics who seem to have been together for quite some time, and this is mainly due to the characters of their bosses, both of whom command immense loyalty.

Matra tends to keep itself to itself with a kind of Gallic disdain, but this is simply a language problem. If you can speak fluent French, you're in; otherwise, *Comment ça va?*" is about as far as one gets. They stay together at the same hotels, eat at an all-French table, mix very little with the rest of the fraternity. Georges Martin, head of the racing department, is the only Matra man I have ever been able to talk to at any length, and he is not exactly a run-of-the-mill mechanic! Maybe they or I will try harder to communicate in the future.

All mechanics, of whatever nationality, have to bear the same hardships and work the same crazy hours. It is not the job for a man who gets homesick or lacks stamina. Jack Brabham summed up the equalities most needed by a mechanic in the following words.

"My idea of a good racing mechanic is one who doesn't try to tell you how good he is; one who is quiet and patient and gets on with the job and doesn't shout about it. He must be thorough, and be able to get himself out of trouble, regardless of what it is. Above all, he must be able to make anything and make anything do—and get that car to the starting line!"

THE CIRCUITS

THE GRAND PRIX CIRCUIT presents an incredibly varied scene to the competitors as they travel from country to country to participate in the thirteen Formula 1 races presently on the Championship calendar.

The first event of the year takes place on the 2.55-mile Kyalami track, situated about fifteen miles outside Johannesburg, South Africa, nearly 6000 feet above sea level, in the undulating bush of the High Transvaal. It is a fast circuit, bare of trees, well-endowed with excellent grandstands but otherwise almost totally without shade. If you have just suffered yet another northern winter, it is with the greatest alacrity that you climb aboard the plane to take you away from the slush and the cold at the end of February!

Letters from Kyalami carry a special postmark—"Escape to Paradise"—and that is exactly how it seems when you arrive in Johannesburg, drive out to the Kyalami Ranch Hotel, which is the most popular and convenient of the hotels in the area, and suddenly find a blue swimming pool edged with bronzed bodies lying out on verdant turf. For a northern European (or an American

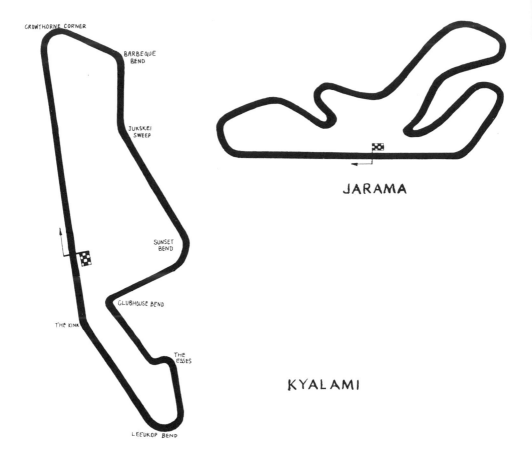

CROWTHORNE CORNER

BARBEQUE
BEND

JUKSKEI
SWEEP

SUNSET
BEND

CLUBHOUSE BEND

THE KINK

THE
ESSES

LEEUKOP BEND

KYALAMI

JARAMA

from Pennsylvania like Mario Andretti), the first instinct is to take off as many clothes as the law allows and plunge into that blue water, then bake under the long-forgotten warmth of that beautiful, beautiful *dangerous* sunshine. . . .

If you are ever lucky enough to experience all this at firsthand, take care. The altitude is such that the ultraviolet rays don't have to work very hard to get to your skin, and it is not so hot that you notice it.

So we arrive at the track the next morning feeling pink, sore and foolish. However, all the drivers agree that Kyalami is one of the best circuits they go to. Some have only known it since the first

World Championship race was held there in 1967, but some have watched it develop since Formula 1 races were first run there in the early sixties, and both groups are impressed. The owners and organizers have made an excellent circuit, and accomplished a lot from the safety point of view. Facilities for spectators, the pit area, the overall organization and the promotion have improved every year. In one driver's opinion, "the people behind it are so much more switched on than most."

Top speed on the straight that passes the pits is now near 180 mph, and the most difficult part of the circuit is considered to be from between Crowthorne Corner right down to Clubhouse Bend. It is a demanding course, up and down hill a lot, and the heat is a factor that has to be carefully considered here with regard to engine, cockpit and driver temperature. But all in all, it is probably the best place of all on the Grand Prix calendar, and everyone looks forward to going there, and returns home with regret.

We move on to Spain in April, one year to the Jarama circuit at Madrid and the next to the Montjuich at Barcelona—two very different tracks. Jarama is a purpose-built race track constructed in 1967, fifteen miles north of Madrid. It is 2.11 miles long, but very twisty. The design is considered a little too tight and too small for Grand Prix racing. Many safety features have been incorporated since its inception, and the access roads are improving, but somehow it never seems to be finished. The "Press Room" is still half full of bags of cement and something will have to be done about the thick dust in the paddock, and the outward flow of traffic after the race. The worst problem, from the Spanish point of view, is that the crowd at Jarama is not big enough. Most people are merely waiting for the evening bullfight!

The Montjuich track at Barcelona is right in the middle of the city, and winds up and down through a wooded park set around the top of a palace-crowned hill. There is a marvelous view of the sea and the shipping, the light and color are magnificent, the city of Barcelona looks very attractive spread out below and across the valley to the next hill, and the facilities are good, as is the weather.

Jack Brabham heads toward the Gasworks Hairpin at Monaco with the buildings of the principality towering in the background.

The track, 2.35 miles long, is like a ribbon of road, lined all the way on both sides with guardrail, and regarded by some drivers as ultra safe, while others think it is no more interesting to race there than on a slot-car set. "It is like racing in a canal," says one prominent driver, "and if you have an accident it is almost impossible not to block the track for other competitors."

However, in 1969 when wing failures put both factory Lotuses out of the race, and Jochen Rindt out of racing for several weeks, it was the lining of guardrails that prevented a Le Mans-type accident, with both cars plowing through spectators standing fifteen to twenty feet deep on each side of the track. The marshaling here was particularly good too.

Monaco is unique. The 1.95-mile circuit is one of the oldest Grand Prix venues still in use, and is the only true "round the houses" race left. I personally think it is out of date, dangerous and would have been discarded long ago if it had not been for the power of sentimentality and the fact that most people like an excuse to go to the French Riviera in May!

The circuit itself is quite a challenge for drivers, and the most exhausting of all from the physical and mental point of view. "By the time you've finished at Monaco you really know you have been driving, from the sheer fatigue you feel. The changing of gears and the twisting of the wheel so many times and for so long is terribly tiring, and the interior of the car becomes very hot because you are never able to go fast enough to get sufficient cooling. The disadvantages of Monte Carlo become greater every year; as the tires and wheels have become wider the track comes to feel narrower. There is less room to maneuver without bumping wheels or hitting curbs, and if you are held up by slower cars there is almost nowhere you can overtake."

That is Jack Brabham's view, a driver who has raced here more

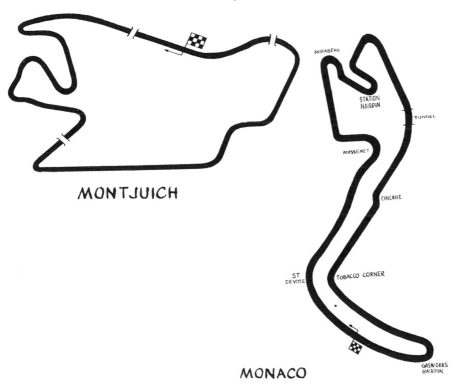

MONTJUICH

MONACO

often than any other; and he feels particularly bitter about Monaco after running straight into the strawbales at the end of the last lap in the lead in 1970, when trying to get past slower cars. But almost all drivers agree that at least the pits will have to be moved from their position, with the cars running along both sides of them. Although it will change the character of Monaco, it is certainly a terrible strain upon anyone in the pits to have this ear-shattering noise going on for two hours with every roar echoed back from the mountains and the skyscrapers and the tier upon tier of buildings which make up the Principality.

This amphitheater, basically natural yet so intensely man-made, is part of the charm of the place, of course. The palm trees, the Mediterranean, the very rich at the Hotel de Paris rubbing shoulders with the humble at the awards presentation, Princess Grace, the countless steps climbing between color-washed villas, the marvelous food at tiny restaurants—it is all still there, but changing.

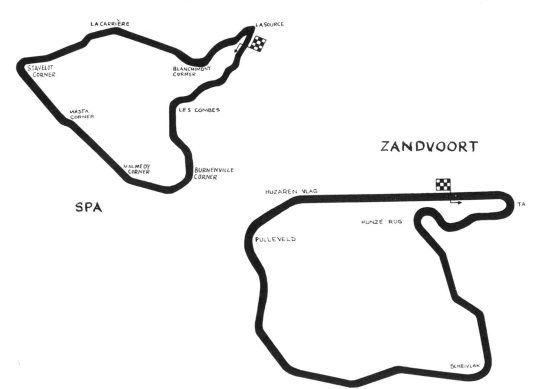

The Spa circuit consists of fast curves and long straights on public highways.

The giant new buildings are spoiling the view, the prices are rising astronomically, Grand Prix racing should take place on circuits built for the purpose, and yet we still go to Monaco. For how much longer, one wonders?

The home of the Belgian Grand Prix, normally our next stop, is, by tradition and use, the course at Spa-Francorchamps. There has been more controversy about this circuit than almost any other in the world. In many ways it is sad that it has become, through increasing speeds, too dangerous for Grand Prix racing. It is set in the Ardennes, a land of forests and hills, very beautiful, very dramatic, very hazardous in the rain. Most drivers enjoy Spa because it is a driver's circuit, very, very fast, with a good surface. It is 8.76 miles long, a series of public roads closed for racing on these occasions, edged with all the usual paraphernalia of ordinary roads—telegraph poles, fences, houses, barns, street lights, curbs, trees and so on. At speeds averaging 150 mph, and in spite of the work that has been done to make it safer, there is still no way you could make it a "safe" circuit for present-day Grand Prix racing. "Providing you stay on the road it is enjoyable!" was one driver's recent comment, while people like Pedro Rodriguez and Jacky Ickx regard it as a pleasant challenge.

I have always dreaded going to Spa since Alan Stacey and Chris Bristow were killed there on the same day in 1960, and there have been many other dreadful accidents before and since. Yet it has a kind of grandeur which I shall miss if the circuit is not used again. Paradoxical.

From Belgium the circus moves on to Holland a fortnight later, to Zandvoort, a small seaside resort on the North Sea coast. The 2.6-mile circuit was built after the war among the German gun emplacements in the sand dunes just outside the town, and it was designed by John Hughenholtz. The whole place has a gay and friendly atmosphere, some good hotels and usually close, competitive racing. Until the death of Piers Courage in 1970, Zandvoort has had a fairly good accident record, partly because there is plenty of runoff space and nothing much to hit. But its greatest drawback is the variable condition of the track surface itself, which

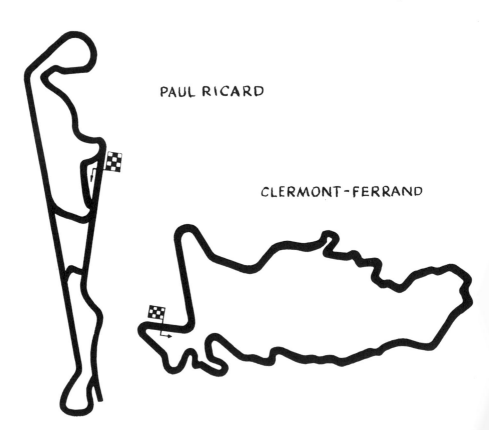

PAUL RICARD

CLERMONT-FERRAND

depends entirely on the weather. If it is windy, which it usually is here, sand blows across the track and, if the weather is also dry, leaves a layer of shifting material that acts like ball bearings between the tire and the track. If it is damp, the roadholding can be very good; if really wet, that introduces yet another problem; sliding off into the sand. And one can always get sand in the throttle slides—or even in the engine.

There is a strong rumor that the land will be sold as real estate and the track will close. In spite of its drawbacks, this would be a great pity, as I think everyone I know enjoys going to Zandvoort. But money has been a problem to the organizers for some time.

The French Grand Prix, the Daddy of them all, has been held on many different circuits, and even now is changing again for the coming year. Reims used to be a regular venue, then Rouen, then Clermont-Ferrand, but there was one rather dreadful excursion to Le Mans, and now we are to be shown the new circuit near Toulon called Paul Ricard. Of all these places I suppose I like the 5-mile Clermont-Ferrand circuit best, though I used to have a soft spot for Rouen—mostly because I knew a fabulous cheap restaurant in the lovely old cathedral city! However, it is clear that Clermont has greater advantages, except that it is more difficult to reach. It is a mountain circuit in the Auvergne region, where spectators can really see some *driving* from their perches on the banks above the track. It is by no means entirely safe, for the road drops away in some places straight down a sheer mountainside, and a car could hurtle over the guardrail and land on the valley floor. It requires a bit of practice on the part of the drivers to learn the long, twisty, up-and-downhill circuit, and its curves have been known to make some of them physically sick from the "g" forces pulling them from side to side as they take the main, fast, tricky, downhill section.

The surface is extremely smooth, perhaps the best anywhere, and although the paddock and pit area need to be entirely redesigned, I can't see why Clermont shouldn't be used permanently as the Grand Prix venue.

The British Grand Prix alternates between Brands Hatch, in Kent, and Silverstone, in Northamptonshire. They are entirely different in every way, and the only linking factor is the organization behind them. Brands Hatch is my "home" circuit, as I have lived very near it all my life, and I have seen it grow from a motorcycle scrambles track to its present position as the biennial home of the Grand Prix of thoroughbred racing cars.

Brands is about twenty miles southeast of London, was originally 1.24 miles long but was extended in 1960 to take in a large area of thin woodland through which an extra 1.4 miles was carved. The circuit is set in a natural bowl of the Kentish hills, and is one of the best spectator tracks anywhere. It is difficult from a driver's point of view and very tiring, while the car takes a bad hammering from the bumpy surface and from the extremes of flat-out running along the straights to sharp braking for the very slow corners on

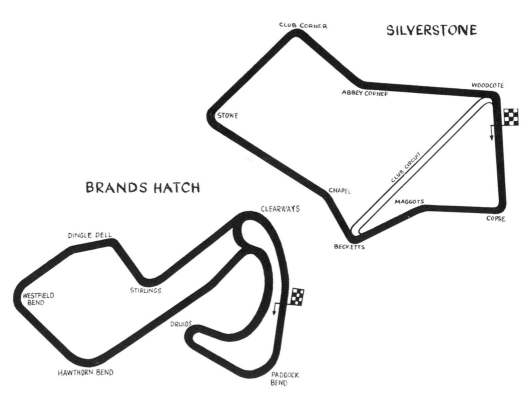

The long straights at Hockenheim make slipstreaming the order of the day.

the oldest part of the circuit. It has reached a point where a good deal of money will have to be spent on it if it is to keep its status. Cars "ground" very badly in at least three places around the track, and at the start of the race a car running with full fuel tanks receives a lot of punishment. It is, in spite of all this, a favorite with many drivers, partly because they know it so well. It is used almost every week of the year for some form of racing, and many British drivers did their first tentative single-seater laps here.

Silverstone is an old airfield. Only the perimeter track (2.93 miles) is now used as a Grand Prix circuit, but just after the war the internal runways were also part of the course. It is flat, featureless, dreadful for spectators but very good from a driver's viewpoint. Silverstone seems to carry tremendous prestige with it for no reason that I can see, but at least they get an enormous crowd considering it really is deep in the country and access roads are badly congested. There is still a lot of work to be done on the safety side to bring it in line with other Grand Prix circuits, but at least it has the crowds, the prestige, the space and the approval of the drivers.

Until 1970 Germany had only one circuit that was even considered for the German Grand Prix—the fabulous, notorious Nürburgring. But the track is narrow, lined with bushes and trees, very long (14.18 miles) and considered nowadays to be very dangerous. If you go off the road at the "Ring" you may not be found for hours. However, most drivers regard it as a place where they can best demonstrate their skill. It may be coming to the end of its long life, but men will still race there if they are allowed to. It runs in steep upward and downward rushes through a section of the beautiful Eifel mountains, and its worst features are the various "Flugplatz" or flying places, and the weather—heavy fogs and rains that descend upon the areas all too often.

In view of the unpredictable weather, the times we have all spent standing in inches of rainwater in the pits, and the obvious dangers to life and limb of driving here in fog, the Grand Prix Drivers Association asked for certain safety measures to be carried out here some three years ago. Time went by, and nothing was done. When it came to 1970 the drivers (not all) said, "No changes, no race." So the Grand Prix was moved, after a lot of drama, to Hockenheim, where it was a roaring success!

The event was a turning point in European Formula 1 racing. Many people will disagree with me, but European road racing in the traditional sense *has* to be on the way out. A great many American ideas, which are even now looked upon as unnecessary and often idiotic by the Fangio-era organizers and journalists, will be gradually adopted over here. I don't mean that we shall have to run all the GPs on banked ovals, or that the old and well loved tracks will have to be abandoned. But change is in the air, change is necessary, change always upsets a lot of people, but change will be for the better. Hockenheim showed the way.

A vast crowd packed into the concrete stadium and the rest of the

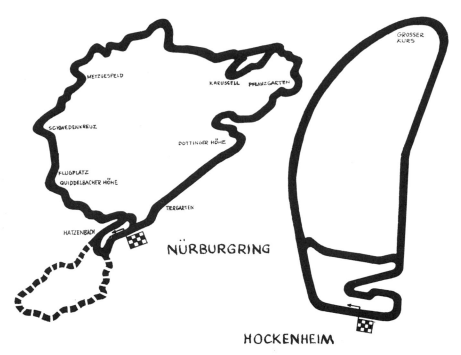

NÜRBURGRING

HOCKENHEIM

4.2-mile circuit was well lined with spectators. It consists, basically, of two long straights between tall, dark fir trees, with a new
chicane in each, joined by a fast curve at one end and a twiddly bit
with sharper corners inside the stadium itself. The concrete bowl
of the stadium holds 120,000 people and looks a bit dismal when
empty, but when the crowd arrives—the only thing like it I have
ever seen is Indianapolis. Everyone enjoyed going to Hockenheim,
and we hope to go back regularly. Those who didn't approve went
to the Nürburgring to watch a Formula 2 event, and missed one of
the best races of the year.

The Austrian Grand Prix cropped up on the calendar for the
first time in six years, mainly because a new circuit, the 3.67-mile
Österreichring, had been built, and partly because of the popular-
ity Jochen Rindt had brought to motor racing in Austria in recent
years.

The Österreichring is set on rising ground above the Mur River,
near Knittelfeld, which isn't near anywhere much. Vienna and

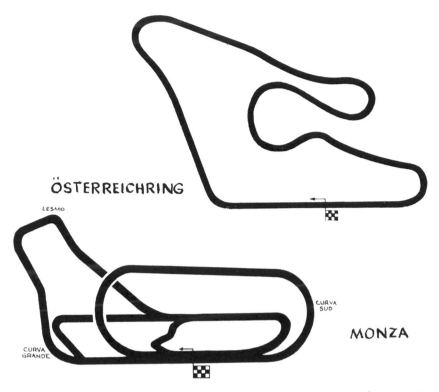

ÖSTERREICHRING

LESMO

CURVA SUD

MONZA

CURVA GRANDE

Graz are quite a long way off in either direction. But the circuit is beautiful, all green in the mountains of Styria, and the minimum speed of every corner is around 100 mph. The surface is good, and drivers were satisfied with safety on the track but not in the paddock. Fans pulled down fences to get to their heroes! Access roads will have to be improved, but there is no lack of enthusiasm or money, although Jochen himself has gone. The Austrian is a good addition to our list of venues. Surtees described it as "a driver's circuit" and was very enthusiastic, and as he doesn't often enthuse, I'll take his word for it.

After Austria most people of leisure move straight on over the Alps to Italy and the heat of Monza, but we have to return to England after *every* Grand Prix to send out photographs and copy to waiting editors. We reach Monza for the Italian Grand Prix each year with a rather "end-of-term" feeling, as this is the last of the

European races before we cross the Atlantic for the final three of the season.

The 3.57-mile Monza circuit is in a park on the outskirts of the town of Monza, near Milano. It is flat, fast and well-known for its slipstreaming battles—which means that cars run close behind one another down the straights, reducing wind pressure until they have built up enough speed to overtake. This can lead to "bunching," which is potentially dangerous as you may have a driver up at the front who would not be there on other circuits, and who is not as competent to cope with the forces involved as his rivals. Jack Brabham calls it "a game of roulette" and says it depends upon how the cookie crumbles on the last lap. It would make more sense if the Italians widened some of the narrow bits of the track and shortened some of the straights. The facilities at Monza, apart from the garages, are a bit rudimentary. The police are officious with those who have every right to be somewhere and not at all concerned about those who haven't. The officials allow far too many people to crowd between the pit road and the track, squeezed between the two rows of guardrails. And the crowd at the end of the race (and before, for that matter) is completely wild, runs all

The Österreichring is a fast, road-type course on the side of a valley.

A group of cars slipstreaming past the pits at Monza.

over the track, and all drivers and pit crews take shelter as soon as possible. It really is frightening.

Later in September we move into the transatlantic phase of the year, going first to Canada, then Watkins Glen and finally Mexico, returning to England between each, unfortunately. One day, we keep telling ourselves, we'll stay over and really see the States . . . one day. . . .

The Canadian Grand Prix alternates between Mosport, 60 miles from Toronto, and St. Jovite, in Quebec province, 90 miles from Montreal. It is difficult to say which is best. Mosport is a friendly place, but very rural, set far away in the country north of Lake Ontario. It is a fairly good circuit (2.46 miles) in the opinion of the drivers, though they complain about lack of facilities to work on the cars. A drafty pit and a canvas tent do not make life any happier for the teams in the cool of early autumn, especially for the mechanics. In a way it is all charmingly amateurish and rustic, especially after the blasé officialdom of Monza and the rest of the older European circuits. But the charm could wear off after a couple of visits. It is a difficult track for a driver, which is what he likes, and the spectators are kept back with good crowd control. Its main disadvantage as a venue is that the hotels are all miles away, and the circus is widely scattered. An enormous Holiday Inn or Howard Johnson's at Tyrone, the nearest village, would be a good plan!

By contrast, St. Jovite is a skiing resort and has everything going for it as far as accommodation is concerned. The countryside is exquisitely beautiful in the fall. However, St. Jovite just does not draw a large enough crowd at present and cannot afford to make needed improvements to the track. The 2.65-mile circuit is *very* rough, bumpy to a dangerous degree, with one or two places where a car can break if it takes the correct line for a corner. The entrance to the pit road is small and, like Mosport, the place lacks

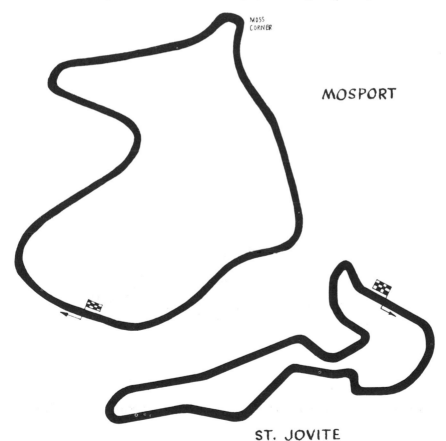

MOSPORT

ST. JOVITE

Mosport is rustic and informal with spectators parking on the hillsides.

facilities for working on the cars. They need somewhere permanent to house them, something like the Kendall Tech Center at Watkins Glen.

I am immensely impressed by Watkins Glen, New York, and I love going there. Everything runs so smoothly, as far as the organization goes, and although I deplore the drafty, damp pits, the quagmire in the paddock and parking lots in time of rain (which seems inevitable for at least one day at each meeting), I like the town and its sense of community, the way it puts on this spectacle and draws such enormous and knowledgeable crowds. It is a Grand Prix I wouldn't miss for anything—and neither would the drivers, with prize money of over $200,000!

I am sure that talking about Watkins Glen as an existing track will be vastly different from how we talk about it after the next GP meeting, because I understand that there are big modifications currently in progress. The circuit is going to be made very much

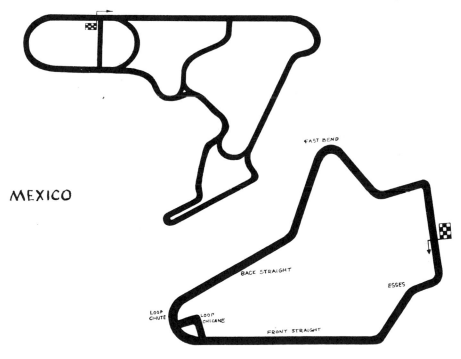

MEXICO

FAST BEND

BACK STRAIGHT

ESSES

LOOP CHUTE

LOOP CHICANE

FRONT STRAIGHT

WATKINS GLEN

The hairpin at Mexico. The circuit is a good one but the spectators are a problem.

wider and I believe they are going to extend the length around the back. It is already a very fast circuit and reasonably safe considering the speeds the drivers achieve there, but at the moment it is too narrow. What the changes will do to the overall lap speed will depend on the way it is laid out. The 1971 double-header meeting (6-Hour race on Saturday, Can-Am on Sunday) should show up all the new virtues of the track itself, just as the 1970 meeting exposed its deficiencies.

In Mel Currie, race director, editor, school board director extraordinare, the Glen has one of its greatest assets. He seems to have infinite patience and goodwill and this inspires those who work with him, from his fellow organizers and directors of the corporation down to the lady helpers in the Methodist Hall. I wish I had seen motor racing in Watkins Glen when the cars hurtled through the streets and the shopkeepers boarded up their windows, but even the new, more sophisticated Glen has a lot of the original parochial quality that makes it unique.

I went to Mexico for the first time in October 1970 all prepared to fall in love with it. Sad to say, my dreams were shattered. Now, I know that was only one visit, and it may all be different in the future, but, oh dear!

The 3.2-mile Autódromo de la Ciudad de Mexico itself is good. Most of the drivers enjoy it, and learn it quickly, although it is fairly difficult to get the best out of it. The Mexicans have made a big effort to bring the place in line with European ones, safetywise; the surface is good, except for one of two areas, but it would be a better place without the banking. Banking is not used on any other GP circuit nowadays, and it puts "g" loads on the car that it is not built to take.

It is an excellent circuit from the facility point of view, having large pit-cum-garages all in one, which makes life much easier for mechanics. The only big disadvantage at Mexico is the people—read on!

THE ORGANIZATION
BEHIND A GRAND PRIX

THERE IS NO DOUBT that the quality and success of a Grand Prix depends very largely upon what has been going on behind the scenes for many months. We all saw in Spain, Great Britain and Mexico in the 1970 season how a meeting can go wrong, for three very different reasons. But all the reasons were related to organization and not to cars and drivers.

In Spain, at the Jarama circuit near Madrid, confusion reigned for almost the entire three days. The Spanish organizers were unfortunate in that they were the first to be expected to implement the new qualifying system. As there were so many competitive cars and drivers at the start of 1970, most European circuits decided that they could not afford them all. Some simply didn't have room for them on their tracks (they said). Monaco has for many years had a sixteen-starters-only rule, and this was extended to some other European Grands Prix. A meeting of organizers and entrants had worked out a strange system whereby all former World Champions and one car from every factory team had a guaranteed entry.

The spectators lining the edges of the track made the running of the 1970 Mexican Grand Prix an exceedingly dangerous proposition.

That made ten. The rest had to scramble for the other six places. As "the rest" were often more competitive than some of the guaranteed starters, there was a lot of bitterness and argument about this new system.

The Spanish race became a fiasco when times were announced as counting for a grid position, and then scrubbed, followed by a decision to let twenty cars race, which was rescinded *on the starting line* and the four extra drivers forcibly removed. Then there was the Ickx/Oliver crash and dreadful fire, which was fought bravely but ineptly by men in shirtsleeeves.

The British Grand Prix, usually run very well, fell down badly in several ways. It seemed that one hand didn't know what the other was doing. First of all there was a mix-up about the fastest practice time and the hundred bottles of champagne that go to the driver who sets it. It had evidently never occurred to anyone that more that one driver might achieve the same fastest time, and no provision had been made for such an event which resulted, tempoparily, in hard feelings between the Lotus and Brabham teams.

Then, the scrutineering was incompetent, bad-tempered and only succeeded in putting everyone's back up. A lot of the officials, although polite to foreigners, became petty tyrants when dealing with the indigenous press and spectator population. And the whole thing was rounded off by a protest at Jochen Rindt's victory, ostensibly because the rear wing was too high, which was proved conclusively to be untrue. Yet the argument went on for two hours before the decision finally went to Jochen and Lotus.

Mexico was something else! No one, but *no one* could control the crowd, not the Clerk of the Course, the local hero, Pedro Rodriguez, or the Mexican police, who looked too young and frightened to act responsibly in any case. The result was the most dangerous race

The paperwork involved in getting transporters of different countries from place to place all over Europe is incredibly complex. Here the transporters have gathered in the paddock at Clermont-Ferrand.

conditions I have ever encountered—in fact, the most dangerous any of the drivers has ever encountered. Dogs, men, women and tiny children ran hither and thither across the track in front of cars racing at 160 mph, they threw bottles and stones, then encroached on the track so far that there was only a narrow tunnel through human beings left for the drivers toward the end of the race. The race only began at all, in fact, because there would have been a riot if it had been canceled. All this, combined with the distinctly shady nature of some aspects of the organization, made the Grand Prix circus vow never to go to Mexico again unless the army lined the track with guns at the ready!

So there you have three distinct kinds of inefficiency at the organizing level. It is important to consider seriously whether those

now in charge of running Grands Prix are qualified to do so any longer. In some cases I think not, and the drivers and constructors mostly agree with me. If a country cannot afford to run a proper Grand Prix, with adequate facilities for all concerned, a safe track and a full, competitive field, then it should not have the privilege of being allowed to stage such a race.

However, to be fair, there is a great deal of work performed in the background by people who get either no reward or very little, except perhaps the satisfaction of having done their own particular task well.

In order to have a Grand Prix at all, a country must be affiliated with the FIA. Delegates from each motoring country form the sub-committee called the CSI, and the countries submit what they hope are acceptable dates for international meetings, of which their Grand Prix will be one, to the CSI during the latter part of each year. The delegates, incidentally, are picked from the most senior and experienced officials of a national motor club.

It is then the CSI's job to sort out a calendar of international events that will please the majority at least, a task that is becoming more difficult as more countries become interested in motor sport. The U.S. has been granted two Grands Prix by 1972, and Australia and Argentina may well be added to the already long list. But some of the older clubs will fall by the wayside as their finances run into a bad patch, or their tracks become out of date.

Once the dates of the coming year's Grand Prix is settled, work can begin at once. Possibly as early as November of the year preceding the race, the design of tickets will have been decided and the work handed over to the printers. The poster may also be designed now, but lately the tendency has been to leave such things, if possible, until the new season's cars have been raced and can be incorporated in the artist's design.

After Christmas the mailing list is dealt with. This consists of the names of some thousands of people who have booked in advance in other years, and, it is hoped, will do so again, giving the club some idea of the hard core of money that will be coming in. There is also

British flag marshals. The blue flag is shown to a car about to be overtaken while yellow flag man turns his back on the race and watches for incidents.

a list of several thousand gas stations, each of whom will receive a poster, a ticket-order form and a prepaid envelope.

One of the big national newspapers, plus, in many countries, the local and often more influential ones, will already have been approached to back the meeting, and it is through their patronage and publicity that most of the better Grands Prix are successful. This is especially true, on a national scale, in England, and on a more local scale in America, Mexico and South Africa. (In some countries one would hardly know, looking around at the nearest city or in newspapers or shop windows, that there was a Grand Prix taking place at all; but these are mostly places which will attract an enormous crowd anyway, on the strength of the national interest in motor racing, as in France, Germany and Italy.)

The regulations and entry forms are sent out to prospective entrants, including foreign teams. Money is now offered on a scale arranged under the Geneva agreement of 1970 whereby all starters are guaranteed a minimum sum, roughly equivalent to their former "starting money," though this is all now described as prize money to give the organizers something to publicize. Starting money used to be the inevitable bête noir of the whole procedure, and caused a good deal of hard feeling between organizers and entrants. The cost to a team of getting two or three competitive cars to every Grand Prix venue rises annually, especially when an Atlantic crossing is involved. The Watkins Glen Grand Prix Corporation, a non-profit body consisting of local people in upstate New York, has always managed to put up the best financial proposition in the world and, along with South Africa, where Alex Blignaut runs the show, they also do a marvelous job of organization in general.

Next, the Secretary of the Meeting, who has usually been through the whole thing many times before and is in charge of all this prerace business, will get in touch with the voluntary helpers who are required, plus the regular police, fire services, ambulance people, security men, program sellers, gatekeepers and so on. Doctors and marshals must be contacted and briefed. The local licensing department applied to for permission to sell drinks outside normal licensing hours. Caterers will put in bids. The public address system may have to be renewed or overhauled, and a firm chosen to deal with this aspect.

Then the television and broadcasting rights—which network will pay the most to handle the Grand Prix? How much coverage will they give it? At what hours will they be using a helicopter, if at all, and when will they want to interview drivers, etc.?

The track itself has to be inspected by a delegate from the Grand Prix Drivers Association, who is one member of the newly formed GP Circuit Safety Committee. Any, some or all of their recommendations for extra safety precautions must be considered and/or met, such as resurfacing, the provision of more guardrails at strategic points or the removal of an earth bank.

Meanwhile the Race Committee has to complete the entry list and send it off to the press, to the fuel and tire and component companies, the latter to help them decide what supplies they will need to cover the whole meeting, which normally lasts three or four days.

Judges are appointed to give official decisions on jumped starts or close finishes, timekeepers to chart every lap and its duration, stewards to ensure that everything is run according to the regulations, scrutineers to see that the cars are "legal," observers to hand in written reports on incidents, accidents or bad driving and, most important of all, the Clerk of the Course, or Race Director. He is the top man in the whole pyramid, he must know every rule in the book, receive reports coming in to Race Control from the marshals throughout practice and the race and make decisions upon them.

About a month before the Grand Prix the programs have to be printed, and the number which will be needed is a difficult thing to assess—their sale often depends upon the weather. Passes are sent out to the press who have requested them (the non-serious have to be weeded out tactfully), photographers' passes are allocated, insurance forms made ready—motor racing is a dangerous business for photographers, too—and passes are issued to teams, sponsors, tire companies and so on. The complaints now begin to pour in, some justified, some not. Car-stickers for the paddock area are very desirable, but at a premium, and mostly reserved for entrants, drivers and officials. However, a lot of other people would like to have one, as they also like to have press passes when not really entitled to them. As for mechanics' passes—they'll turn up on the arm of almost anyone, from a ravishing blonde model to a seven-year-old schoolboy.

The Press Officer has one of the most difficult and diplomatic jobs of all, coping with the desires and demands of foreign reporters and photographers more easily than with his own countrymen. For example, when a spotty young lad from a local weekly paper wants to be able to go out onto the track on equal terms with the regular, well-known carefully selected members of the International Racing Press Association, what can the Press Officer do? Only be firm in the face of abuse.

At some Grands Prix the press facilities are *very* poor, either from the point of view of queueing up to collect passes, or having interminable waits for time sheets to be completed, or providing enough telephones, or just being generally difficult. Watkins Glen, Kyalami, Zandvoort and Austria are without doubt the best places to be a member of the press, Germany and Monaco the worst. Spain alternates between the luxury of Barcelona's facilities and the virtual nonexistence of those at Madrid.

The drivers and teams generally enjoy Kyalami most, because "everything just happens" and there are no great dramas. Spain and Mexico they could do without, and Monza always brings far more than its share of tension and panic. Both Canadian races tend to be friendly, pleasant affairs but a little rustic—teams like proper garages to work in—Watkins Glen is popular with mechanics and the press but not so much with members of the team who have to put up with the miserable pit area. (This is in the process of being changed, I know.) Any Grand Prix in France is liable to be fairly well-run as long as nothing interferes with lunch, and no one says *Merde* to a policeman!

But to be really serious, I must say something about the marshals. Their place may eventually be taken by "traffic lights," signals hung out over the track to give drivers instructions. Until this becomes a worldwide method, the flag marshals have one of the most responsible jobs in motor racing. Great Britain is fortunate in having a dedicated, well-trained corps of flag marshals who have received praise from drivers of every nationality; but in every country they have to be enthusiastic and dedicated men to endure the long hours, the often miserable conditions of wet or cold and the few thanks they receive.

At each marshals' post around the track there will be two flag marshals and a fire marshal, the latter equipped (one would like to think invariably) with the latest in fire-resistant clothing complete with helmet and face mask such as a spaceman might wear, and the rescue equipment to deal with any fire emergency. There will also be someone to man the telephone that links the post with Race Control, and course marshals ready to deal with accidents or

Whole lengths of fences were pushed down by spectators at Mexico in 1970.

track clearing operations. And there will be one observer.

Of the two flag marshals, one is in charge of the blue flag and one the yellow. The "blue" is shown to any oncoming driver who is about to be overtaken by a faster car. The "yellow" alerts the marshals at the next post and warns the drivers of any mishap between the two posts. If the yellow flag is waved vigorously it means there is great danger ahead, if held still it means, more or less, "Watch it, hazard ahead." It is forbidden to overtake when the yellow flag is out, and anyone who does so is brought in by the Clerk of the Course and reprimanded, at the least.

A yellow and red striped flag means that there is oil on the track, and the same "yellow" marshal is also in charge of the white "ambulance (or other service vehicle) on the track" flag. The "blue" marshal always keeps his eye on the overtaking situation.

The black and the red flags are in the charge of the Clerk of the

99

Course, who will use his own judgment as to when they must be used. The "red" means "stop immediately." The "black," shown with a board with a number on it, means that the driver of the car carrying that number must come in at the end of his next lap. This is usually for some infringement of the rules, for dropping oil, or because the car has been reported as being in a dangerous condition. The national flag of the country concerned is usually used to start a race, and the black and white checkered flag to signify its end.

There are also pit marshals and paddock marshals, whose job it is to keep everything running smoothly in either place, and to bring order to any situation which may look potentially dangerous or stupid. Without these men, no race meeting of any kind could take place, and for a Grand Prix the country's finest marshals are assembled.

The other side of the coin altogether is the work done by a competing team before a Grand Prix; I don't mean the making of the cars or the testing of tires, but the apparently simple matter of making sure that cars, drivers and mechanics all arrive at the right place at the right time. This is usually the unsung work of someone back at the factory, stuck in the office with a telephone and a typewriter. She (often this work is left to a woman) needs to book a garage for the cars in the vicinity of the track, as in Europe garages are not always provided *at* the track. Then she must book hotel accommodations for the mechanics, for the drivers, for the team manager and probably for the constructor/entrant/big boss himself.

For a European race, if the team is British-based, she has to book the transporter onto a cross-channel ferry, and that is not easy in the summer months for something as big as a transporter. The worst chore of all, wherever the cars are going, is the documentation. There has to be a complete list of the spares the mechanics will be taking with them to a race that may be several weeks ahead. This information is needed for a document called an *Acquit à Caution* that is absolutely necessary if the transporter is going into

France and coming out again, as it so often is. Then the team has to have carnets from the FIA for each individual racing chassis, each engine, and for the vehicles which will be carrying them. If the transporter is going through Germany, Spain or Switzerland a more detailed carnet is needed from the London Chamber of Commerce. And for Spain it is essential to have a special permit from the Spanish transport ministry, *plus* the provision of an insurance bail bond to prevent the mechanics being thrown into jail if there is a road accident! In France one also needs a "Road and Bridges Permit," and in Italy yet another "special permit." The inability to produce any or all of these may delay the transporter for days, as has often been known to happen, especially at the Spanish and Italian borders.

The team must be sure the mechanics have international driving licenses, that their passports are still valid, that they have current American or Mexican visas, and that their smallpox certificates are up to date. The provision of enough money to cover all foreseeable circumstances is another problem, especially on the long Canada/United States/Mexico visit.

So, you see, the organization problems are not all on one side. To bring a Grand Prix before the public takes a lot of people a lot of time, worry and expense. It must be worth it, or I wouldn't be writing this book.

THE WOMEN
BEHIND THE MEN

THE GIRL WHO LOVES a racing driver has a tough time. Of course, the rewards can be great, both in terms of her man's personality and his income. More often than not she has a very ordinary background and finds herself—especially if she picks a potential winner and marries him—with material assets she never expected to obtain. But she pays for them; believe me, she pays!

She must be—or become—a rather special sort of person if she is to make a success of being a racing driver's wife/girlfriend/mistress. She has to come to terms with danger, first of all. The girl who makes a fuss in the paddock before the race and kisses her driver "goodbye" with tears in her eyes won't last two minutes. Scenes are out. Neither must she go to the other extreme and wish him luck with excessive gaiety. She must, in fact, be elsewhere, preferably in the pits with a job to do. The wives of most Grand Prix drivers are to be seen throughout practice sessions and race days, come wind and high water, imminent or recent childbirth,

Greeta Hulme   **Helen Stewart**

sitting hunched on the pit counters of the world working at stop-watches, time sheets and lap charts with distilled concentration. It is useful. And it is necessary, both to the success of the team and to the wife's nervous system.

For the watching woman, a race can be intolerable without work. If she is unable or unwilling to pitch in with the general effort she would be well advised to stay at home. The men love to have the pits draped with decorative females during practice, but with a race on there is nothing worse than a non-contributory body among the signal boards, the heaps of tires, the jacks and the tool boxes. (When the mechanics start to trip over you, you have more than overstayed your welcome and should beat a hasty retreat.)

The worst time for the woman who loves a racing driver is the start of a race. On race day itself she wakes up with that awful

103

sinking feeling that always precedes something one wishes were over. She probably finds her man sleeping heavily, almost defiantly, until a fairly advanced hour. To eat, or not to eat, is a personal matter with both drivers and wives, but most do not, especially at the hotter venues. Coffee and Coca-Cola are the most popular forms of sustenance on race days. If she is really in love with her driver, as opposed to having gotten used to him, even coffee tends to choke her. If she is wise, she dresses and gets out of the bedroom and leaves him in peace, for his temper won't be any too good today.

In the early days of his career, a driver will want to go to the track as soon as possible and tinker with the car, and his girl has to go along too, and hang about for hours with nothing whatever to do but exchange talk with other women in the same boat. But as a driver climbs the ladder of success he will time his arrival later and later to avoid crowds and autograph hunters, and to enjoy a little more leisure and privacy at his hotel. This is preferable. The buildup of tension is compressed into a shorter time.

The wife or girlfriend working in the pit goes along to take up her position at least half an hour early. She is usually dressed in slacks and a loose shirt for high temperatures, a thick sweater and an anorak for low. It is very dirty on a race track. She expects to get her hair filled with rubber dust and her face covered with grime of every sort, and she chooses her clothes accordingly. Her man may turn his head to watch a girl in a figure-hugging dress pass, hip-swaying along the pit apron with a great big "Mechanic" pass on her arm, but he'll think his woman a fool if she turns out in similar style.

Now the cars form up on the grid, and the crowd shouts and the emotional temperature begins to rise. I defy anyone connected with racing not to be affected by this excitement, especially when the engines start and work up to their crescendo. Then the flag is dropped and a cloud of rubber dust is all that the anxious eyes in the pits can see as the cars roar away out of sight. For the driver's woman it is probably the only moment when she prays, even if she has been hardened to the whole procedure over the years. Then she settles down to her job, knowing that this is the pinnacle of his life, his *raison d'etre*, and that whatever happens now is out of her control. The race becomes almost commonplace as she ticks off lap after lap.

If she is worth her salt, she has to be unaffected by the "oohs" and "ahs" of the crowd, by other people coming into the pits and by the commentary. She is a member of a team. Even if her man's car does not come around, she must go on pressing her stopwatch, or logging the times, or charting numbers. If she loses track, all her effort is wasted, and she has let the team down.

What goes through a woman's mind when the man she loves is missing? She would be odd, indeed, if her stomach did not turn over and her heart skip a beat. But she does not have hysterics on the pit counter. She does not run around the track to find out what has happened. She presumes he is all right; he has pulled off the road, is walking back.

And, usually, he is. She begins to breathe properly again when he comes into sight, and he may spare her a brief glance of reassurance. He may look cross, or sheepish, or merely hot and dirty, but he wanders back as if it were all in a day's work—and it is. If the girl is new to racing she may think the worst, straight off, when he doesn't come around on time, because she hasn't learned how often things can go wrong with a car without any harm to anyone. Maybe she is the dramatic type and is more in love with the idea of being in love with a racing driver than with the man behind the goggles. This happens often, but these girls do not usually last the season out.

Obviously a woman has to learn to live with the fact that her man's profession is a fairly dangerous one, but she doesn't talk about it. Maybe, once in a lifetime—that would be enough. More difficult to swallow, perhaps, are the other hazards attendant on life with a racing driver. The other women, primarily; lots of women, young, pretty, willing. If a wife is possessive she may have a very agonizing time, even if she has no actual cause for jealousy. She

105

Pat Surtees   **Nina Rindt**

may not be able to stand the competition and just give up, leaving the field free for the "girl-at-every-circuit."

Or she may set her jaw and never let her driver out of her sight, which works very well if there are no children to consider. As soon as she has a baby, her loyalties are divided, and she cannot fly around the world with so much ease. Quite often she has to let her man go alone to such exotic places as Mexico, Monte Carlo, South Africa, knowing that there are parties and dancing and girls. She's either got to trust him and shut up about it, or assume he's going to be unfaithful and acccept it. Or leave him. Some have done just that.

It isn't only other women that can split a racing marriage. Some wives can't stand living out of suitcases. Some resent being overshadowed by a husband's strong personality. And make no mistake about it, at home the top racing driver comes first, last and all the time; he has to, or he would not be what he is. He may be the most charming of men, generous, humorous, a wonderful lover, but he is inevitably an egotist of the first order.

In this respect the mistress has the advantage over the wife. She need only see the best of her man. She is not there when he has a tantrum over a meal that isn't ready when he wants it or a shirt that hasn't been ironed. But in other ways she has the toughest time of all. Not for her the victor's kiss after the race. Not for her the place of honor beside him at the celebration dinners. And, most difficult of all, she mustn't bat an eyelid if he crashes. The woman in love with the married racing driver makes herself a bed of roses —complete with thorns.

Those who do not really understand what it entails, often cite foreign travel as being the most glamorous and enviable part of the motor racing life. This is partly true. It is very pleasant to be in Monaco in May, in Italy in September and the eastern United States in October. Each venue has its atmosphere and its beauty, the hotels are usually the best, the food is varied and good, comfort and service are taken for granted.

But against this you have to set the monotony of air travel, the pressure of time limits for getting from place to place, and the fact that one is seldom at home, where things are familiar and comfortable. In addition the circus involves the same set of circuits year after year, with scarcely any variation, so that one may get to know Monte Carlo, Zandvoort, Monza, Mexico City, etc., very well indeed, and yet be completely ignorant of the everyday life of the countries involved.

English is spoken everywhere in a greater or lesser degree, and it is quite possible for a driver to travel 100,000 miles in a year without speaking a single foreign word if he does not wish to. This insularity, which is partly forced on him by people anxious to help and shield him from difficulties, grows as his stature grows. The first-year Formula 3 driver and his wife/girlfriend probably have a lot more real fun doing the thing on a shoestring and camping out in a converted truck at Monaco, for instance, than "the head

107

that wears the crown" staying at the Hotel de Paris. But success always brings a certain amount of sacrifice, and you can't have it both ways. (Be sure you're the kind of girl who can take changes in stride, and won't pine too much for the days when you laboriously painted numbers on his Lotus Seven.)

Which brings me to the question of ambition. While a woman naturally wants her driver to win, she is less ambitious than he. That is not to say unambitious—she likes the fame and fortune and glamour of being a champion's wife, and, of course, he's much better tempered when he wins! But, for some, his presence in the pit, safe and tangible, is more important—there's an odd mixture of disappointment and relief in every woman who watches her driver retire from a race.

Another word of warning: a girl may find it useful, when it comes to understanding what they never stop talking about, to have taken a course in Advanced Motor Engineering, or some such. But don't bother to air your knowledge. Even if you can design a Grand Prix or an Indy car to beat all comers they'll never listen to a word

Catherine Ickx   **Maria-Helena Fittipaldi**

Donatella de Adamich

you have to say on the subject. They know best. So just nod in the right places and they'll think you're adorable.

Conversely, if you don't know a camshaft from a crankshaft, never mention either. They are intelligent men, in the motor racing game, and you will give them a pain if you pipe up with some imbecile remark in the middle of an earnest technical discussion.

Yes, they're intelligent men, and attractive men, and very highly geared professional men. Life with a racing driver is full of excitement, stress, separation, boredom and exasperation. In view of this it is, perhaps, surprising that so many racing marriages are so successful. One reason may be that the women involved are indeed exceptional, with plenty of will power. Another is that in such an itinerant, event-filled life, it is essential for the driver to have an anchor and a refuge, even if he feels it cramps his style at times. On the top rungs of Grand Prix racing the same faces have been around for quite a while. The pattern of each relationship is a little different from the other naturally, but not all that much.

And there is one thing on which all racing wives are agreed— they would not want their husbands to do anything else. The men they fell in love with are not nine-to-five types and never will be. The spark would go out of them if they were prevented from following their star, and the spark is what makes them different from other men.

109

THE POLITICS
OF GP RACING

I'M NOT REFERRING to party politics; in the context of motor racing the term means negotiating for money, contracts of one kind or another. And the money factor becomes more important every year, which, with a worldwide recession going on, makes it ever more difficult for a team to field Grand Prix cars.

It costs about $120,000 a year to make and race one GP car for a season, and the bulk of this has to be guaranteed before the year begins if possible. It has been the policy of the tire and fuel companies to support teams and/or drivers in return for a guarantee that their product will be used exclusively for the length of time agreed in the contract. Usually the company receives a lot of good publicity in return, and it also gives them a chance to try out new products on the race track, gaining valuable experience that can be passed on to the general public, the everyday car drivers.

This $120,000 per car estimate is for a team building its own car—if you buy a car from someone else it is obviously cheaper—

Chris Amon's STP March Ford is a mobile decal display.

but that amount just about covers all your budgeted expenses of running a car for a season without including the capital expense of the engines. It doesn't take into account the return from a race meeting; how much you get back in this way is just a gamble, so you can hardly include it in the annual budget. Teams have to get most of this money from somewhere that is 100 per cent certain, as they are not gamblers at heart. This figure does not include driver's fees either, so a team needs sponsors to cover the driver's fees *and* a large proportion of the cost of the car.

The amounts that tire and fuel companies will provide varies with every team and with the state of the economy. In the past Dunlop, Goodyear and Firestone have been very generous, and the fuel companies of Shell, Esso, BP, Gulf and Elf have been the other major sponsors. Now most of these have cut back expenditures drastically, if not pulled out of Formula 1 racing altogether, and teams are having to look elsewhere, outside the "trade," for their money.

A certain amount of money comes from the component com-

The Goodyear service area at Monaco.

panies that provide brakes and brake linings, ignition systems, spark plugs and so on, but this is on a bonus basis and amounts to very little—a few hundred dollars, maybe, for winning a GP. There is little front money—some free parts, but not all.

At the moment it is the tire companies that teams and drivers woo extensively from the time of the Canadian Grand Prix onward, if there is the possibility of a new contract in the offing. It is one of the more amusing sights during the latter part of the year, to watch quietly and see who is talking to Leo Mehl of Goodyear and who to Bob Martin of Firestone, with that hungry look in their eyes! Dunlop backed Jackie Stewart and Ken Tyrrell in Formula 1 for three great years, and Jackie repaid them marvelously with his many appearances for Dunlop, his inevitable mention of the company in speeches and by winning the World Championship in 1969. Unfortunately, although Dunlop is not closing its racing division, they have pulled out of Formula 1—for a while, at least. This leaves Goodyear and Firestone with the added burden of the Tyrrell and BRM teams, and although there has been much talk of Michelin coming into racing, we have seen no concrete evidence of this yet. (Ferrari was testing Michelin tires in Austria after the

112

Grand Prix, but nothing seems to have been settled between the two companies.)

Firestone is cutting back drastically this coming season, and if it were not for Andy Granatelli and his STP backing, the March company might have been in very bad straits.

Fortunately for BRM, the cosmetic firm of Yardley came into motor racing sponsorship in a very big way at the beginning of 1970, and spared no expense to influence an enormous potential male market that is beginning to regard "Yardley for Men" as a reality and not just a slogan. This is all to the good and the way we in motor racing would like to see things go. A few years ago, advertising, sponsorship and decals were very much frowned upon by the European purist, the amateur race-goer and by the majority of the press. It is, in fact, an American idea that we used to fight against and now welcome with open arms.

The first outside company of any size to show the way over here was Players (cigarettes), which took the Lotus cars for their own and renamed the team "Gold Leaf Team Lotus." It was a bit startling at the time, and received all kinds of criticism, but those who were against this kind of change had no idea of the mounting ex-

The Yardley mobile home in the paddock at the Österreichring.

Most of the Dunlop tires at the 1969 Mexican Grand Prix were air freighted in at considerable expense even though Dunlop had already won the championship.

pense of racing, or of the mutual advantages of big sponsorship. Without it, international motor racing would be virtually dead by now.

Brooke Bond Oxo (bouillon and tea) put some money into Rob Walker's 1970 venture with Graham Hill—indeed, Rob was one of the very first to go out and seek sponsorship and put decals on his cars. There was a ridiculous row during the 1968 British Grand Prix because the BBC (British Broadcasting Company), which is non-commercial, refused to televise the event unless all decals were removed. This cost Rob alone over $2000 in one weekend.

What Europe needs is sponsorship on an American scale, like Reynolds Aluminum has given Team McLaren. It is time the Grand Prix teams stopped sneering at the weird and wonderful names given to Indianapolis cars because of their sponsors—without them, Indy would be a very dull and poverty-stricken affair.

Newspaper combines, national airlines and tobacco companies have all dabbled their toes in motor racing, but it is for the Grand Prix teams that we need more support. Come in textile companies, chain stores, mining concerns, electrical firms, syndicates. We need your help.

114

WHAT IT IS
ALL ABOUT

THE END PRODUCT of all this feverish activity is, of course, a race; to be exact, a Grand Prix counting toward the world championships for drivers and for constructors. After the designing of the car comes the prototype, and after that the testing. Some teams test their cars exhaustively before taking them to a race meeting. Some are paid by the tire companies to track-test a new compound. Goodwood, Silverstone, Zandvoort and Kyalami are busy places both during and out of season, while Lotus has its own test track at Hethel beside the factory, which can be used whenever necessary. Tire testing at Kyalami is a very popular chore that is carried out in January or February, when Europe and North America are not the nicest places to be living!

The other Formula 1 races, like the Race of Champions at Brands Hatch, the International Trophy Meeting at Silverstone and the Oulton Park Gold Cup are looked upon mainly as pointers to the season's potential outcome or as a kind of show window for new or modified cars. There is a small amount of money in each,

The sunshine and the pool at the Kyalami Ranch Hotel are a welcome sight at the start of each season.

and a good slice of prestige if you win, but they are part of the preparation for the twelve or thirteen major tussles that the Formula cars have during the year.

When the circus is off on its travels, it is remarkable how often we all meet for the same flight out of London Airport, especially early in the year. There may be Colin Chapman, Jackie Stewart, Graham Hill, Denny Hulme, Ken Tyrrell, Ron Tauranac, Jo Siffert, Chris Amon, Rolf Stommelen, François Cevert, Robin Herd, some of the tire company personnel, some mechanics, some press. It depends where we are all going. For some of the nearer European races, Colin Chapman and Jack Brabham have always flown their own light planes, and Ken Tyrrell has recently taken to hiring a plane for his team. But some of the longer flights are made interesting by the company, and shop talk is the order of the day.

We tend to stay at the same hotels year after year—unless they are torn down, as happens at Monaco! And we tend to stay together, so that each evening there are informal dinners after practice which may involve one team, or a mixture of drivers, managers and writers at the same table. We chew over the events of the day, try not to be drawn back to the garages to see how the cars and mechanics are getting on, but very often pay them a late night call out of curiosity and friendliness—or dire necessity, if you happen to be running the team.

At Monaco this involves four different visits around the crowded Principality, maybe more. BRM, Ferrari, McLaren always use individual garages there, while Lotus, Brabham, Matra, March and Tyrrell gather in one giant one just behind the first row of hotels and offices opposite the pits and the harbor.

At Spa, Belgium, teams are scattered all over an area of several miles so we usually have a good, slow meal in the evening, get up and out of the hotel early and stay at the track all day. One cannot do that at Monaco, because the track is closed for the minimum possible amount of time, and traffic and people flow freely as soon as the barriers are cleared to form small gates.

Zandvoort is a good place to stay, with almost everyone, including trade representatives and mechanics, staying at either of two hotels, with the vast garage used by most teams. This is one place where the late night call is all part of the itinerary, and often includes a walk by the sea before going to the hotel to write up the day's practice story.

For the French race we usually stay within the same town at least, and have our favorite hotels. If we want to see anyone in particular we know where they are staying and can go around for a coffee after dinner.

There are often evening functions that almost everyone in the circus attends, but the number of these varies with each country. The awards presentations are sometimes fun, and worth attending. Sometimes we have to leave before they take place anyway. Sometimes they are a bore, and given a severe miss by all concerned!

"Functions" vary from cocktail parties where everyone stands for ages with a glass and a canapé, to beery get-togethers where the band plays so loudly you have to shout at each other all the time.

117

There is also the Elf party in Monaco every year, where they show a marvelous film on three separate screens at once. And the South African Automobile Club dinner in Johannesburg which is a bit stuffy, prim and proper, and no one dares to get involved in a discussion in case the question of race and color is raised. There is also the quite incredibly fabulous awards presentation in South Africa which takes place on a Sunday morning in the private home of a leading citizen—gorgeous food, swimming pool, tables with umbrellas casting welcome shade, total informality.

It is hardly fair to single these out, because every country does something in the way of hospitality, the United States and Mexico being among the best. Some of the old fun days have gone forever, I fear—the champagne chateau party near Reims where servants, carrying lighted flambeaux, lined the long, long drive to the incredible, fairy-tale castle, for instance. . . .

But all these relaxations come after a very hard day's work. We are at the track from immediately after breakfast until long after practice has ceased, in order to wait for times to be printed and issued. Then we drag ourselves back to the hotel for a shower—or preferably a long, soaking bath—before we go to dinner, usually our only proper meal of the day.

In between the rolls and coffee of the morning and dinner at night, we have a variety of jobs to do. I, personally, go from pit to pit checking on situations, who changed an engine last night, and so on, go to chat with the tire company personnel, maybe tape an interview with a driver, then get down to the serious business of timing. I usually time for one particular team, not necessarily the same at each meeting. In this way I am being useful and keeping in touch with events on the track.

The photographers wander off to find the best vantage points from which to take their pictures, and if it is fine, take as many photos as possible while the light is good in case it changes drastically the next day. But, of course, race pictures are a separate consideration, and it is just too bad if the day is a gray one for the big event itself.

Last-minute drama—Lotus mechanics change an engine in less than two hours between a Sunday morning practice session and the start of the race.

Some journalists trot up and down writing notes in their little books, jotting down times, recording dramatic events on the track, and the pit stops, and what they are for. All this is necessary for writing up a full report of the meeting later, even, for some magazines, down to chassis and engine numbers. Changes in tire compounds are noted and discussed, any modification, any minute change in a wing angle. I'm afraid I am not so minutely technical, but I do keep a very keen eye on the goings-on, and try to see the wood instead of the trees, if you understand me.

Meanwhile, the teams are doing everything they know to put up some fast times in case the weather breaks. There is often a lot of pit activity on the first day of practice, and maybe gear ratios have to be changed, or an engine blows out on the track, or a driver dents his car more than a little. It is a day of experiment, unless

119

the team has sneaked in a day or two of unofficial practice prior to the first official session.

This is often the case, and sometimes proves to be the right time for me to be there, because that is when I get my chance to go around each track with a driver—maybe Jackie Stewart, maybe Jacky Ickx or Clay Regazzoni—whoever happens to ask me! This is wonderful for my appreciation of the circuit, and the driver's problems in negotiating it. The only Grand Prix circuit I have never been around is Monza. The police don't let you.

Official practice sessions vary in duration and distribution with each organizing club, and they can be frustrating, restricted matters of half an hour, which isn't enough, to four hours without a break, which is a bit too much—at least for those who sit keeping a stopwatch on about ten or a dozen cars at once. If you are working for a team obviously you have to record every lap of their one, two or three cars, but you must also be able to tell the team manager at any second just who, out of the whole field, is fastest, or what the lap record was during last year's practice. So you sit tight on a heap of tires and a piece of foam plastic, and hope someone remembers to bring you a cup of coffee sometime.

Practice days must look very strange to a spectator. It is quite usual for a driver to be in and out of the pits with his car every lap or two, and maybe he doesn't get in a single flying lap until quite late in the day. (A standing lap is one which he started from the pits, from a standstill, and the first flying lap is the one from which you can begin timing as he speeds past the pits out on the track.) If he is unhappy about the handling, the ride, the steering, the seating position, the oil pressure, the number of revs he is getting in top gear, the driver will be in to talk it over with his team manager and chief mechanic. Then he may climb out of the car, remove his helmet and lie out on the pit counter for a rest, or wander along to see what the opposition is up to. Or he may, though this is getting rarer, work on the car himself.

There was an attempt to bring the Indianapolis style of qualifying to Grand Prix racing, in which one car at a time is allowed

The tension and pressure have built to a climax as the cars are on the grid. Then at the fall of the starter's flag, men and machines charge off in search of the checked flag.

out on the track for three or more flying laps, but it didn't work. Practice for Formula 1 cars begins and ends at specific times, and there are usually one or two sessions on each of two or perhaps three days of official practice. As soon as the starting line marshal waves the green flag or switches on the green light, anyone who is ready and rarin' to go is out of the pits onto an empty track. Times are usually slow at first, but as the day comes to an end, anything up to twenty seconds may have been dropped from the morning's lap times, and the really fast boys try to outdo each other in the last ten, or even five minutes. This used to be one of Jack Brabham's favorite habits—he'd wait to see what everyone else had done, and then go out just as the man was looking for the checkered flag and knock several tenths of a second off the best time! Nowadays it is more likely to be Jackie Stewart, Jacky Ickx or Clay Regazzoni who will take up the last-minute challenge.

It is very rare for the pole position to be decided on the first day, though it has happened even this year. It is much more usual,

To be victorious, to be the winner, to be—at least on this day—the best there is, that is what it is all about.

weather being good, track conditions not too oily, and the car and the driver still game, for the pole to be decided by computer, because the cars and drivers are so closely matched that there is often not as much as a second between the fastest and the tenth fastest car. Therefore we all hang about after the last session of practice on the evening before the race to make quite certain of the grid positions when we receive the official, printed sheet of times.

After the grid has been decided, either in three-two-three or two-two formation, depending upon the width of the circuit, the drivers can do nothing about it but wait for the starter's flag. There is usually some kind of big party the night before the race, and most drivers and teams make an appearance, even if they creep out around 11 P.M. in order to get a reasonable night's rest. No one makes a big thing about this early night business nowadays, and some drivers may be night-clubbing or watching over their

122

engine change until after midnight. But there is definitely no play-boy "eat, drink and be merry" attitude either. As for myself, I creep out of parties, too. Race day is a very hard and long one for the press, and usually we have to leave for the dash to the airport to catch an evening flight back home the minute the race is over—dirty, tired, maybe upset, carrying lap charts, notebooks, cameras, luggage and wondering where to dump the rented car.

On race morning the first thing we check is the weather. Then we have a Continental breakfast in Europe and a hearty egg-and-bacon one elsewhere; this is mainly because the French, Italians, Germans, et cetera, take forever to come up with anything but rolls and coffee, and it is usually Sunday, and they think we are all mad to forego a three-hour lunch for a motor race anyway. But it is partly because in South Africa, Canada, the U.S. and Mexico you are expected to eat well in the mornings, and the meal is served quickly, with a "You're welcome," and it makes *so* much difference. I lose weight drastically by simply not eating throughout the European season, and put it all on again in the fall!

We almost always feel a bit edgy on race day. People may not admit it, but anyone with a modicum of sensitivity will be hoping for a trouble-free race above all things, and a tiny bit scared that it won't be. My husband spends ages getting his many cameras loaded and ready for use, and we don't have much to say to each other for once. Sometimes he goes to the track very early, while I stay on at the hotel and get a lift to the track later with whichever team I am helping at the time. We have had some amusing and hair-raising experiences getting to the track with a couple of drivers at the last moment, blasting our way past the queueing public, and having arguments in basic Anglo-Saxon with the foreign police. Jochen Rindt used to swear violently at them and drive on in a cloud of dust, Jackie Stewart uses charm and persuasion up to a point, but even he gets to the swearing stage quite quickly on race day. Everyone has his own way of expressing the tension that is inevitable when there is about an hour to go before a Grand Prix.

The mechanics are usually having some last-minute drama in

the pit or paddock, "Who's taken the —— fire extinguisher? Where are those —— overalls, the *clean* ones? No, we haven't got any stickers!" Or else there's a grim and ominous hush, and you creep past the mechanics and hide away in a corner until it is time to climb onto the pit counter and take up station for the race.

The excitement builds as the spectators fill the grandstands. The engines start firing up as the last scrutineering is over, the cars are fueled and the tires are decided upon once and for all—one hopes. A lot depends on the look of the weather. This year was a good one, but some seasons are raincoat and rubber-boot years, and not amusing. A dry, sunny day with enough breeze to keep everything cool is ideal. We rarely get that.

When the band has finished playing, the parade of drivers is over, and the last-minute dash to the appropriate toilet (if any) has been accomplished, the drivers put on all their protective gear, climb into their cars and set out on the "warmup" lap, stopping about one hundred yards behind the start line at the dummy grid. The latter is a fairly recent innovation, brought in to reduce the chances of starting-line incidents. The cars form up in starting order while mechanics top up the tanks with fuel, make minor adjustments, even cope with last-minute crises like the replacement of a battery or ignition box. Then the one-minute signal is given, the engines are started, the track is cleared and the cars move forward to the grid proper.

The last minutes before a race begins are a strain on the nerves. The men in the cars are no longer the men I swam with in the pool yesterday, or had dinner with last night, or joked with this morning. They are shut up in their private world, closed away from us by a helmet and a visor; a man and his machine, charged with adrenalin and fuel, waiting for the moment of truth.

Their eyes are on the starter and his flag, their cars in gear and engines revving. The noise reaches a crescendo and they pass the pits in a haze of tire smoke and a blur of color. There isn't a thing I can do to help any one of them then, except keep the lap chart for the team; so I stop chewing my pencil and get down to work

The winner's moment of glory—champagne and the silver trophy.

with absolute concentration, eyes fixed on the corner before the pits to see who comes around first.

After that, anything may happen. Nothing is settled until the checkered flag falls. A driver can build an enormous lead only to have his fuel pump fail or his gearbox seize. The winner may seem an absolute certainty as they begin the last of 28, 60, 80 or maybe 100 laps, depending on the circuit. But after twelve years of Grand Prix racing I never, never remark or predict until I see that leading car take the flag, and watch the rest of the finishers come over the line—or straight into the pit.

There have been wildly joyful moments, with champagne in a big silver bowl passed around the team. There have been times of absolute despair when you go away in tears swearing never to go near a motor race again—yes, and I'm not the only one who can weep. I've seen the strongest, most arrogantly masculine drivers and team managers in tears too. And there have been times when the result of the race has been a big surprise, or even hilariously

125

funny, as when four consecutive leaders ran out of fuel at Spa one year. It is an unpredictable, sad, happy, rather crazy, totally absorbing world.

Someone said to me last week, "I think all the *passion* has gone out of motor racing." Oh, rubbish. We are less amateurish than when we began, less "shoestring," more used to big hotels and traveling in jet planes, we have had more disappointments and more triumphs; we are definitely older! But there is plenty of passion left in motor racing.

All the time there are new drivers, new cars, even new teams coming into the Grand Prix world, and being just as successful, certainly faster, than their predecessors of the fifties and sixties.

People sometimes say they envy me because I travel the world, enjoy my work *and* get paid for it. Well, as I said at the beginning of this book, I consider myself lucky, although the stresses are great, the travel tiring. We never get to see much of any country except its race track, and we shall never be rich. But we are involved in a great sport, which is completely international, with no class distinction *at all*, the whole circus consisting of people with Personality with a large P. And that is why I love it.

WINNERS

Since the World Driving Championship was inaugurated in 1950, thirty-five drivers have won Grands Prix. They are:

MARIO ANDRETTI

American, 1 Grand Prix win
b February 28, 1940

Mario Andretti was born in Trieste, Italy, and his family moved to the United States in 1955 when he was fifteen. Always fired with enthusiasm about motor racing, Andretti helped convert a Fiat 500 into a single-seater special with a group of other young teenagers before he moved to the other side of the Atlantic.

He soon became involved with American motor racing, first with small midget racing cars on small ovals and then with the big USAC National Championship machinery. In 1965 he finished third in the Indianapolis 500-miler at his first attempt (behind Jim Clark and Parnelli Jones) and went on to win the championship. He finally won Indianapolis in 1969, while he gained the championship title in both 1966 and 1969.

127

Andretti first drove a Formula 1 car in 1968. In the U.S. Grand Prix at Watkins Glen he shocked everyone by taking pole position from the Grand Prix regulars and then holding second place until the front bodywork started to break up. Not much success followed with Lotus cars in 1969 and Marches in 1970, but Andretti's first call was USAC Championship racing and he was unable to take part in all the Formula 1 Grands Prix.

Joining Ferrari for 1971, Andretti won the first championship race of the year, the South African Grand Prix, and later added the non-championship Questor Grand Prix in California to his tally.

Grand Prix win:
1971 South African Grand Prix, Kyalami   *Ferrari*

ALBERTO ASCARI

Italian, 13 Grand Prix victories
World Champion 1952 and 1953
b July 13, 1918; d May 26, 1955

Son of the famous Alfa Romeo Grand Prix driver Antonio Ascari, Alberto Ascari couldn't help but follow in his father's footsteps. (Antonio was killed racing at Montlhéry, France, in 1925 when Alberto was only seven.) At the age of eigh-

128

teen, Alberto first raced a 500cc Sertum motorcycle in 1936, winning a works ride for Bianchi the following year.

Ascari's debut on four wheels came in the 1940 Mille Miglia when he drove the first-ever Ferrari, the 815, leading the race until it broke down. After the war, Ascari immediately made a name for himself driving Maserati and Ferrari cars. His most successful seasons were in 1952 and 1953 when he won six out of seven and five out of eight races respectively to claim the World Champion's crown both years.

Little success followed in 1954 with Lancia—apart from victory in the sports car Mille Miglia—and the following year he was killed testing a Ferrari sports car at Monza. Ironically, this occurred only four days after a most spectacular accident in the Monaco Grand Prix when Ascari had escaped unhurt after his Lancia plunged off the road into the harbor.

Grand Prix wins:

1951	*German Grand Prix, Nürburgring*	*Ferrari*
	Italian Grand Prix, Monza	*Ferrari*
1952	*Belgian Grand Prix, Francorchamps*	*Ferrari*
	French Grand Prix, Rouen-les-Essarts	*Ferrari*
	British Grand Prix, Silverstone	*Ferrari*
	German Grand Prix, Nürburgring	*Ferrari*
	Dutch Grand Prix, Zandvoort	*Ferrari*
	Italian Grand Prix, Monza	*Ferrari*
1953	*Argentine Grand Prix, Buenos Aires*	*Ferrari*
	Dutch Grand Prix, Zandvoort	*Ferrari*
	Belgian Grand Prix, Francorchamps	*Ferrari*
	British Grand Prix, Silverstone	*Ferrari*
	Swiss Grand Prix, Bremgarten	*Ferrari*

GIANCARLO BAGHETTI

Italian, 1 Grand Prix win
b December 25, 1934

Giancarlo Baghetti could be likened to a rocket: he leaped suddenly into prominence, had a tremendous win and then crashed downward to fade completely from the scene.

He first raced his Alfa Romeo road car at Monza in 1957; by 1959 he was driving an Abarth sports car and in 1960 he conducted a Lancia-engined Formula Junior Dagrada. Ferrari had promised to loan a Formula 1 car to the most promising up-and-coming Italian in 1961. Baghetti was chosen.

In his first race, the non-championship Syracuse Grand Prix in Sicily, he trounced the factory Porsches of Dan Gurney and Jo Bonnier; then he won the similar-status Naples Grand Prix and was entered in the French Grand Prix at Rheims. It was a fairytale ending, with the factory Ferraris dropping out and Baghetti saving the day with a surprise win in his first-ever world championship event!

Thereafter Baghetti had little success and at the end of 1962 left the Ferrari team to join the ATS stable. He had no luck and apart from a few one-off drives up until 1967 Baghetti disappeared from the Formula 1 scene. He later took up motor racing journalism and photography.

Grand Prix win:
1961 French Grand Prix, Reims-Gueux   *Ferrari*

130

LORENZO BANDINI

Italian, 1 Grand Prix win
b December 21, 1936; d May 10, 1967

Lorenzo Bandini started as a garage mechanic at the age of fifteen and like most Italian boys dreamed of racing cars. At the age of twenty he had his own garage business and in 1957 he had his first taste of competition, hillclimbing his friend's Fiat 1100.

By 1958 Bandini was taking part in Formula Junior racing, being Italian Champion in 1959, and in 1961 he was invited to drive Formula 1 and Intercontinental Cooper Maseratis for Guglielmo Dei's Scuderia Centro-Sud team. In 1962 he joined Ferrari, but the Italian team was disorganized at that time and he did not race in every event. Dropped in 1963, he drove a privately entered BRM for Scuderia Centro-Sud and put up such sterling drives that Ferrari brought him back onto their team by the end of the year!

Bandini drove for Ferrari from then until his fiery accident in the 1967 Monaco Grand Prix. Gravely injured, he died three days later. Bandini's single Grand Prix win was in Austria in 1964 on the rough and bumpy Zeltweg airfield circuit.

Grand Prix win:
1964 Austrian Grand Prix, Zeltweg   *Ferrari*

JOAKIM BONNIER

Swedish, 1 Grand Prix win
b January 31, 1930

Sweden's Jo Bonnier, son of a Professor of Genetics, started rally driving at eighteen. At twenty-three, after a spell in the Swedish navy, he took up ice racing with a $3\frac{1}{2}$-liter Alfa Romeo and three years later, in 1956, he had his first drive in a Grand Prix car.

Driving for BRM in 1959, Bonnier won the Dutch Grand Prix to score the British marque's first-ever Grand Prix win. It was Bonnier's first and only Grand Prix win; in fact, it was the only time he has ever featured in the first six either before or since. He drove for Porsche in 1961 and 1962 and then switched to Rob Walker's private Formula 1 team to drive Cooper and Brabham cars in 1963, 1964 and 1965. From 1966 he has run his own Grand Prix cars—Cooper, Brabham, Lotus and McLaren models—but has never been among the front-runners.

Most of Bonnier's success in recent years has been in sports car racing, notably with Lolas, and most of his publicity comes through his presidency of the controversial Grand Prix Drivers' Association.

Grand Prix win:
1959 Dutch Grand Prix, Zandvoort   *BRM*

Bonnier   **Brabham**

JACK BRABHAM

Australian, 14 Grand Prix victories
World Champion 1959, 1960 and 1966
b April 2, 1926

When Jack Brabham retired from motor racing at the end of 1970, aged forty-four, he was still in peak form and a potential winner of any race. His racing career spanned twenty-three years, from the time he raced dirt-track midgets in Australia in 1947.

In 1955 he went to England and soon found a place on the Cooper team, making his Grand Prix debut with an outclassed Cooper Bristol in the British Grand Prix at Aintree that year. By 1957 he was regularly competing in Formula 1 races in what were basically Formula 2 Coopers with slightly enlarged Climax engines; two years later these "baby" cars had grown up into world-beaters and, taking two victories, one second, two thirds and a fourth, Brabham took the world championship narrowly from Tony Brooks and Stirling Moss.

Many people said the shy Australian was lucky, so in 1960 he bagged five of the season's nine races to claim the title by a convincing margin. In 1962 he left Cooper to build his own cars and in 1966 won the world championship yet again, the first man to do so in a car of his own manufacture. After the 1970 Mexican Grand Prix Brabham announced his retirement and took his wife and family back to Australia.

Grand Prix wins:

1959	Monaco Grand Prix, Monte Carlo	Cooper Climax
	British Grand Prix, Aintree	Cooper Climax
1960	Dutch Grand Prix, Zandvoort	Cooper Climax
	Belgian Grand Prix, Francorchamps	Cooper Climax
	French Grand Prix, Reims-Gueux	Cooper Climax
	British Grand Prix, Silverstone	Cooper Climax
	Portuguese Grand Prix, Oporto	Cooper Climax
1966	French Grand Prix, Reims-Gueux	Brabham Repco
	British Grand Prix, Brands Hatch	Brabham Repco

133

	Dutch Grand Prix, Zandvoort	Brabham Repco
	German Grand Prix, Nürburgring	Brabham Repco
1967	French Grand Prix, Le Mans au Bugatti	Brabham Repco
	Canadian Grand Prix, Mosport Park	Brabham Repco
1970	South African Grand Prix, Kyalami	Brabham Ford

TONY BROOKS

British, 6 Grand Prix wins
b February 22, 1932

Very quiet and shy, Tony Brooks hit the headlines in 1955 when he won the non-championship Syracuse Grand Prix in Sicily driving a British Connaught. He defeated the might of the Maserati factory team, and it was his first race in a competitive Formula 1 car! Aged twenty-three, he was a student dentist who drove as a hobby.

His first race had been in 1952 in a Healey Silverstone and very soon he graduated through a Frazer Nash to a 2-liter Connaught single-seater. In 1956 he was invited to drive for BRM, but the cars were unreliable and Brooks had a bad crash at Silverstone when the transmission locked up. In 1957 and 1958 he drove for Vanwall, notching up four wins, and in 1959 Brooks joined Ferrari, for whom he scored another two wins.

After that Tony's career seemed to take a downward trend. He raced for the Yeoman Credit Cooper team in 1960, with little success, and in 1961 drove for BRM. After a miserable two years he retired from racing at twenty-nine for family reasons and to run his garage business.

Grand Prix wins:

1957	British Grand Prix, Aintree	Vanwall
	(car taken over by Moss)	
1958	Belgian Grand Prix, Francorchamps	Vanwall
	German Grand Prix, Nürburgring	Vanwall
	Italian Grand Prix, Monza	Vanwall
1959	French Grand Prix, Reims-Gueux	Ferrari
	German Grand Prix, Avus	Ferrari

134

Brooks   **Clark**

JIM CLARK

British, 25 Grand Prix wins
World Champion 1963 and 1965
b March 4, 1936; d April 7, 1968

Jim Clark won more Grands Prix than anyone else. By winning the South African Grand Prix in January 1968, he recorded twenty-five victories, one more than Juan Manuel Fangio. Three months later the apparently indestructible Scot was killed when his Lotus plunged off the road into some trees in a minor Formula 2 race at Hockenheim, Germany. He was thirty-two.

Clark's winning streak started in 1962 when he won the Belgian Grand Prix on the extremely fast 8.76-mile Francorchamps circuit. He was unlucky not to win the world championship that year, for he was leading in the final race, the South African Grand Prix, when a plug in the engine unscrewed itself, oil leaked out and Clark's race was over while his close rival Graham Hill went on to win. In 1963 he won seven of the season's ten races (a record number for any year) to clinch the title comfortably. In 1964 he won three races to the two of Surtees, but Surtees took the title through scoring several place results—if Clark didn't win, it was usually because he had broken down! Clark won the championship again in 1965, winning six of the season's ten events, but in 1966, the first year of the 3-liter Formula 1, Lotus hadn't a competitive car. Clark's Ford-engined Lotus took four races out of eleven in 1967 to the two victories of Denny Hulme, but Hulme got the verdict as he had scored more points through netting place results than Clark had in victories.

A shy Scottish farmer, Clark became interested in motor racing after watching an event in Ireland at the age of fifteen. In 1955, aged nineteen, he participated in rallies and in 1956 and 1957 took part in a few small Scottish club races with road cars. In 1958 he raced a D-type Jaguar in some major meetings and from then onward never looked back. Clark was supreme from 1962 to the time of his death.

Grand Prix wins:

1962	*Belgian Grand Prix, Francorchamps*	*Lotus Climax*
	British Grand Prix, Aintree	*Lotus Climax*
	U.S. Grand Prix, Watkins Glen	*Lotus Climax*
1963	*Belgian Grand Prix, Francorchamps*	*Lotus Climax*
	Dutch Grand Prix, Zandvoort	*Lotus Climax*
	French Grand Prix, Reims-Gueux	*Lotus Climax*
	British Grand Prix, Silverstone	*Lotus Climax*
	Italian Grand Prix, Monza	*Lotus Climax*
	Mexican Grand Prix, Mexico City	*Lotus Climax*
	South African Grand Prix, Kyalami	*Lotus Climax*
1964	*Dutch Grand Prix, Zandvoort*	*Lotus Climax*
	Belgian Grand Prix, Francorchamps	*Lotus Climax*
	British Grand Prix, Brands Hatch	*Lotus Climax*
1965	*South African Grand Prix, Kyalami*	*Lotus Climax*
	Belgian Grand Prix, Francorchamps	*Lotus Climax*
	British Grand Prix, Silverstone	*Lotus Climax*

	French Grand Prix, Clermont-Ferrand	*Lotus Climax*
	Dutch Grand Prix, Zandvoort	*Lotus Climax*
	German Grand Prix, Nürburgring	*Lotus Climax*
1966	*U.S. Grand Prix, Watkins Glen*	*Lotus BRM*
1967	*Dutch Grand Prix, Zandvoort*	*Lotus Ford*
	British Grand Prix, Silverstone	*Lotus Ford*
	U.S. Grand Prix, Watkins Glen	*Lotus Ford*
	Mexican Grand Prix, Mexico City	*Lotus Ford*
1968	*South African Grand Prix, Kyalami*	*Lotus Ford*

PETER COLLINS

British, 3 Grand Prix victories
b November 1931; d August 3, 1958

Fair-haired Peter Collins, the son of a motor distributor, started motor racing at the age of seventeen with a 500cc motorcycle-engined Formula 3 Cooper. He quickly made a name for himself in this form of racing, which assisted many newcomers in the late 1940s and early 1950s. By 1952 he was driving Formula 2 cars for HWM. He later drove for Aston Martin, Vanwall, BRM and then Ferrari.

In 1956 he came very near to winning the world championship after a successful year driving Ferraris, but in the Italian Grand Prix, the final event of the year, Collins handed his machine over to Juan Manuel Fangio, his team leader, whose Ferrari had broken down. The great Argentinian was therefore assured of his fourth world title.

Two weeks after winning the British Grand Prix in 1958, Collins crashed his Ferrari heavily in the German Grand Prix. He was taken to hospital with severe head injuries, but died the same day. He was twenty-six.

Grand Prix wins:

1956	*Belgian Grand Prix, Francorchamps*	*Ferrari*
	French Grand Prix, Reims-Gueux	*Ferrari*
1958	*British Grand Prix, Silverstone*	*Ferrari*

LUIGI FAGIOLI

Italian, 1 Grand Prix victory
b 1898; d June 20, 1952

Luigi Fagioli belonged to the Old School. His long career began in 1926 with an 1100cc Salmson. Before World War II he was a member of the famous Hitler-backed Mercedes-Benz and Auto Union Grand Prix teams.

Although he retired from racing in 1938 because of ill health, in 1950 he returned, driving an 1100cc Osca sports car to class victory and an amazing seventh overall in the Mille Miglia. The result was that he was invited to join Farina and Fangio on the all-conquering Alfa Romeo Grand Prix team in 1950 and 1951. His one win was in the 1951 French Grand Prix, shared with Fangio who took over Fagioli's car when his own machine broke down.

Fagioli crashed his Lancia Aurelia saloon practicing for a sports car race at Monte Carlo in 1952. The fifty-four-year-old veteran died three weeks later from his injuries.

Grand Prix win:
1951 French Grand Prix, Reims-Gueux   *Alfa Romeo*
*   (car taken over by Fangio)*

JUAN MANUEL FANGIO

Argentinian, 24 Grand Prix victories
World Champion 1951, 1954, 1955, 1956 and 1957
b June 24, 1911

Perhaps the greatest racing driver ever, five times World Champion, Juan Manuel Fangio was the son of an immigrant potato farmer. Since he started work as a mechanic at the age of eleven he always dreamed of racing cars. At twenty-five he was a riding mechanic and then two years later, in 1938, he raced his own Ford Special.

By 1948 Fangio was a hero in Argentina. Backed by the government, he came to Europe to race a Simca Gordini at Reims, France, but the car let him down. He returned in 1949 and, driving Maserati and Ferrari cars, took Europe by storm. In 1950 he was invited to drive for the factory Alfa Romeo team; the following year he was World Champion.

In 1954 and 1955 Fangio took the championship for the second and third times, this time driving for Mercedes-Benz, who had returned to motor racing triumphantly after their famous prewar successes. In 1956 Fangio switched to Ferrari and, although un-

139

happy in the team, took the title yet again. His 1957 season, high-lighted by a sensational win in the German Grand Prix at Nürburg-ring driving for Maserati, was his last full one and for the fifth and last time Fangio claimed the world championship.

Saddened by the deaths of many of his friends in racing accidents, Fangio retired halfway through the 1958 season at the age of forty-seven. Since then he has helped to organize motor racing in Argentina, where he is a wealthy businessman, and he is still a famous figure around the world's circuits.

Grand Prix wins:

1950	*Monaco Grand Prix, Monte Carlo*	*Alfa Romeo*
	Belgian Grand Prix, Francorchamps	*Alfa Romeo*
	French Grand Prix, Reims-Gueux	*Alfa Romeo*
1951	*Swiss Grand Prix, Bremgarten*	*Alfa Romeo*
	French Grand Prix, Reims-Gueux	*Alfa Romeo*
	(took over Fagioli's car)	
	Spanish Grand Prix, Pedralbes	*Alfa Romeo*
1953	*Italian Grand Prix, Monza*	*Maserati*
1954	*Argentine Grand Prix, Buenos Aires*	*Maserati*
	Belgian Grand Prix, Francorchamps	*Maserati*
	French Grand Prix, Reims-Gueux	*Mercedes-Benz*
	German Grand Prix, Nürburgring	*Mercedes-Benz*
	Swiss Grand Prix, Bremgarten	*Mercedes-Benz*
	Italian Grand Prix, Monza	*Mercedes-Benz*
1955	*Argentine Grand Prix, Buenos Aires*	*Mercedes-Benz*
	Belgian Grand Prix, Francorchamps	*Mercedes-Benz*
	Dutch Grand Prix, Zandvoort	*Mercedes-Benz*
	Italian Grand Prix, Monza	*Mercedes-Benz*

Fangio   **Farina**

1956	Argentine Grand Prix, Buenos Aires	Ferrari
	(took over Musso's car)	
	British Grand Prix, Silverstone	Ferrari
	German Grand Prix, Nürburgring	Ferrari
1957	Argentine Grand Prix, Buenos Aires	Maserati
	Monaco Grand Prix, Monte Carlo	Maserati
	French Grand Prix, Rouen-les-Essarts	Maserati
	German Grand Prix, Nürburgring	Maserati

GIUSEPPE FARINA

Italian, 5 Grand Prix victories
World Champion 1950
b October 30, 1908; d June 29, 1966

Son of the eldest of the Farina brothers who founded the famous Turin coach-building firm, Giuseppe "Nino" Farina was a doctor of law. The first-ever official World Champion in 1950, he survived several nasty motor racing accidents. He retired in 1956 but was killed in a road accident ten years later at the age of fifty-seven.

Farina started motor racing in the 1930s—he was Italian Champion in 1937, 1938 and 1939—and after the war raced his own Maserati. He drove for Alfa Romeo in 1950 and 1951 and then joined Ferrari for 1952 and 1953. His 1954 season was punctuated by serious accidents in the Mille Miglia and Monza. In 1956 he went to Indianapolis to drive an American car in the 500-mile race, but when another driver was killed testing the machine he finally decided to give up the sport he loved.

Farina's trademark was his relaxed, arms-out driving style. This was copied by many of the younger drivers, notably Stirling Moss, and is common practice today.

Grand Prix wins:
1950	British Grand Prix, Silverstone	Alfa Romeo
	Swiss Grand Prix, Bremgarten	Alfa Romeo
	Italian Grand Prix, Monza	Alfa Romeo
1951	Belgian Grand Prix, Francorchamps	Alfa Romeo
1953	German Grand Prix, Nürburgring	Ferrari

EMERSON FITTIPALDI

Brazilian, 1 Grand Prix win
b December 12, 1946

Sensational is the only way to describe Brazilian Emerson Fittipaldi's impact on the European motor racing scene. Now aged twenty-four, he is currently the youngest driver regularly competing in Grand Prix racing. As leader of the Lotus team, he has the difficult job of trying to continue the successes of the late Jim Clark and the late Jochen Rindt and already he has one Grand Prix to his name, the 1970 U.S. event.

In Brazil Fittipaldi, whose elder brother Wilson also races, had an enormous reputation which started from the age of fifteen when he raced 50cc motorcycles. He later raced karts, saloon cars, GT cars and sports cars before leaving for Britain in 1969 to race a Formula Ford Merlyn.

Fittipaldi was an overnight sensation, graduating into Formula 3 in mid-season and winning the championship despite his late start. In 1970 he raced a Formula 2 Lotus, finishing third in the European Trophy, but in mid-season he was already in Formula 1.

One of the brightest hopes in motor racing, Fittipaldi is not a hot-headed youngster. The Brazilian drives in the cool, calculated manner of a World Champion.

Grand Prix win:
1970 U.S. Grand Prix, Watkins Glen   *Lotus Ford*

142

RICHIE GINTHER

American, 1 Grand Prix win
b August 5, 1930

Californian Richie Ginther only won a single world championship race, the last of the 1½-liter Formula 1 races in Mexico in 1965 driving a Honda. But he was a reliable driver, someone who usually finished a race. His record of eight seconds and five thirds backs this up.

A friend of Phil Hill from Hill's early MG days, Ginther worked as a mechanic. His first real taste of motor racing came in 1953 when he was passenger to Phil Hill in the Pan-American road race. They crashed, but Ginther came back for more the following year when Hill finished second.

By 1957 Ginther was driving Ferraris himself. Three years later he was offered a contract with Ferrari, so he resigned from running a Ferrari agency in the United States and came to live in Europe. He joined BRM in 1962 as number two to Graham Hill and left to go to Honda in 1965; in 1967 he teamed up with Dan Gurney on the Eagle team, but after failing to qualify to start in the Monaco Grand Prix he suddenly announced his retirement from racing. Today he is often involved with the running of racing teams in the United States.

Grand Prix win:
1965 Mexican Grand Prix, Mexico City   *Honda*

143

JOSÉ FROILÁN GONZÁLES

Argentinian, 2 Grand Prix victories
b 1922

Burly José Froilán González, nicknamed the Bull of the Pampas as he was renowned for his "charging" early in his career, was somewhat overshadowed by his fellow countryman Juan Manuel Fangio. Eleven years Fangio's junior, González came to Europe in 1950 and drove privately entered Maserati and Ferrari cars.

In 1951 he was invited to join the Ferrari team and his most notable and heroic drive was at Silverstone where, at the age of twenty-nine, he hurled the big $4\frac{1}{2}$-liter Ferrari Grand Prix car round the aerodrome circuit to beat Fangio's Alfa Romeo. It was not only Ferrari's first world championship win, but also the first time the Alfa Romeo had been defeated for several years. His second Grand Prix win was also at Silverstone, in 1954.

After a serious accident at the end of 1955, González only made one more European appearance before going into semi-retirement in Argentina where he now runs a large Chevrolet agency.

Grand Prix wins:

1951 British Grand Prix, Silverstone	*Ferrari*
1954 British Grand Prix, Silverstone	*Ferrari*

DAN GURNEY

American, 4 Grand Prix wins
b April 13, 1931

The son of an opera singer, Dan Gurney's first race was in a Triumph TR2 in California in 1955. A Porsche 1600 followed, then a 4.9-liter Ferrari sports car with which Gurney had tremendous success. He raced three times in Europe in 1958, but with little success, although he showed sufficient speed to impress Ferrari team manager Romolo Tavoni. With Mike Hawthorn's re-

Gonzáles   **Gurney**

tirement in late 1958, Gurney had a test drive for Ferrari and by mid-1959 was a member of their Grand Prix team.

Gurney joined BRM in 1960, then changed to Porsche for 1961 and 1962. His first Grand Prix win came in 1962 at Rouen, scene of the French Grand Prix. It was Porsche's only Grand Prix victory. A switch to the Brabham team was made in 1963 and then in 1966 Gurney decided to follow his team leader and build cars of his own, known as Eagles. In 1967 Gurney won the Belgian Grand Prix driving his V12 Eagle, but the following year engine troubles decided Gurney to quit European Grand Prix racing.

Gurney himself retired from active racing in the middle of 1970 to concentrate on running a team of his own Eagles in American racing.

Grand Prix wins:
1962 French Grand Prix, Rouen-les Essarts   Porsche
1964 French Grand Prix, Rouen-les-Essarts   Brabham Climax
*   Mexican Grand Prix, Mexico City   Brabham Climax*
1967 Belgian Grand Prix, Francorchamps   Eagle Gurney-Weslake

145

Hawthorn   **G. Hill**

MIKE HAWTHORN

British, 3 Grand Prix wins
World Champion 1958
b April 10, 1929; d January 22, 1959

Mike Hawthorn was Britain's first World Champion in 1958. In a peculiar set of circumstances he only won one race to Stirling Moss' four and Tony Brooks' three, but because he had accumulated more points through gaining several place results he won the title by the narrow margin of one point over Moss. Three months after gaining the title and officially announcing his retirement from racing, Hawthorn was killed in a car accident in Britain. His Jaguar 3.4 went out of control, hit an oncoming truck and smashed into a tree.

Hawthorn first made a name for himself in 1952 at the age of twenty-three; he raced a Riley in small club meetings, but at Goodwood on Easter Monday he appeared with a brand new Formula 2 Cooper Bristol and trounced everyone. Continued successes led to his inclusion in the Ferrari team in 1953 and he astounded everyone by beating none other than Fangio after a wheel-to-wheel battle in the French Grand Prix at Reims.

146

After unsuccessful attempts to get the British Vanwall and BRM cars competitive in 1955 and 1956, Hawthorn returned to Ferrari for 1957 and his championship year, 1958. He was also a successful sports car driver, notably with the famous D-type Jaguar, but although he won the 1955 Le Mans 24-hours, his victory was overshadowed by the tragic disaster which claimed eighty-one lives. Some people tried to blame Hawthorn for the accident—he had slowed to come into the pits at the time and possibly helped to start a chain reaction which sent another car hurtling into the crowd—but an official inquiry cleared him.

Grand Prix wins:

1953 French Grand Prix, Reims-Gueux		*Ferrari*
1954 Spanish Grand Prix, Pedralbes		*Ferrari*
1958 French Grand Prix, Reims-Gueux		*Ferrari*

GRAHAM HILL

British, 14 Grand Prix wins
World Champion 1962 and 1968
b February 15, 1929

One of the best-known racing drivers today is Graham Hill. World Champion in 1962 and 1968 and runner-up in 1963, 1964 and 1965, he is now forty-two but shows no inclination toward retiring. Anyone who might have written him off as a topliner got a shock after his first few drives for the Brabham team in 1971. This came just over a year after he had made a tremendous comeback to racing in March 1970 following a bad accident in which he injured his legs in the U.S. Grand Prix in October 1969.

Hill got into motor racing as a mechanic. He helped prepare other drivers' cars in return for an occasional ride himself. By 1956 he was racing factory Lotuses and two years later was a member of the then new and inexperienced Lotus Grand Prix team.

In 1960 Hill joined BRM and two years later won his first championship race, the Dutch Grand Prix, in the new V8 BRM. He ended the year winning the championship. In 1967 he rejoined Lotus as teammate to Jim Clark; early in 1968 Clark was killed, but Hill restored team morale by winning the world championship again. In 1970 he drove Rob Walker's privately run Lotuses and after Walker's withdrawal at the end of the year switched to Brabham for 1971.

Graham Hill has also scored wins in many other classes of racing, from simple touring machines to big sports cars. In 1966 he won the richest race in the world at his first attempt, the Indianapolis 500.

Grand Prix wins:

1962	*Dutch Grand Prix, Zandvoort*	*BRM*
	German Grand Prix, Nürburgring	*BRM*
	Italian Grand Prix, Monza	*BRM*
	South African Grand Prix, East London	*BRM*
1963	*Monaco Grand Prix, Monte Carlo*	*BRM*
	U.S. Grand Prix, Watkins Glen	*BRM*
1964	*Monaco Grand Prix, Monte Carlo*	*BRM*
	U.S. Grand Prix, Watkins Glen	*BRM*
1965	*Monaco Grand Prix, Monte Carlo*	*BRM*
	U.S. Grand Prix, Watkins Glen	*BRM*
1968	*Spanish Grand Prix, Jarama*	*Lotus Ford*
	Monaco Grand Prix, Monte Carlo	*Lotus Ford*
	Mexican Grand Prix, Mexico City	*Lotus Ford*
1969	*Monaco Grand Prix, Monte Carlo*	*Lotus Ford*

PHIL HILL

American, 3 Grand Prix wins
World Champion 1961
b April 20, 1927

The first—and so far the only—World Champion from the United States, Californian Phil Hill claimed his title in 1961 when he drove for Ferrari. This was the first year of the 1½-liter Formula 1 and Ferrari was the only team to have truly competitive cars, so the outcome of the championship was decided between the Italian team's two star drivers, Hill and German Wolf-

gang von Trips. They started the Italian Grand Prix virtually level on points. On lap two von Trips' Ferrari collided with Clark's Lotus, the German driver being killed in the accident. Hill's world championship was therefore automatic if he won the race; he did, but it tasted bitter.

Hill was a product of the American club racing school. His success with privately owned Ferraris led to occasional invitations to join the factory team in 1955 and 1956. By 1957 he was a permanent member of the sports car team and in late 1958 he was driving in the Formula 1 team.

Hill was a very "nervy" driver—he suffered a lot from ulcers—and he did not get on with Ferrari politics and left the team after a miserable 1962 season to join the rival Italian ATS team. This team was a failure, so Hill joined Cooper in 1964, again with unsuccessful results. Hill was still extremely successful in sports car racing, however, until he finally hung up his helmet in 1967.

Grand Prix wins:
1960	*Italian Grand Prix, Monza*	*Ferrari*
1961	*Belgian Grand Prix, Francorchamps*	*Ferrari*
	Italian Grand Prix, Monza	*Ferrari*

149

Hulme   **Ickx**

DENIS HULME

New Zealander, 5 Grand Prix wins
World Champion 1967
b June 18, 1936

Denny Hulme's story is a rags to riches epic. He had been a successful driver in New Zealand, first driving an MG in 1956, and he came to Eurpoe with George Lawton under a "Driver to Europe Scholarship" in 1960. Driving Formula 2 and Junior Coopers he was reasonably successful, but considerably saddened by Lawton's death in a Danish race.

His first Formula 1 drive, in a Yeoman Credit Cooper Climax at the end of 1960 at Snetterton, was originally intended for Lawton, but given to Hulme after the accident. Subdued, he was fifth. He campaigned a Formula Junior Cooper in 1961, but with no success, and continued with it in 1962, also working for Jack Brabham as a mechanic. He raced a Brabham Junior a few times and was sufficiently impressive to be offered the factory car (which he also prepared) in 1963.

By 1964 Hulme was racing Formula 2 Brabhams and had an outing in a Formula 1 car in a Swedish non-championship event.

150

In 1965 he was offered more drives and the following year he was Jack Brabham's regular number two.

Suddenly Hulme had arrived. He won the Monaco Grand Prix in 1967 and later claimed two more races plus the world championship, beating his boss Jack Brabham and Jim Clark. The following year he moved to Bruce McLaren's team, winning the Italian and Canadian Grands Prix and being well in the running for the world title. Following McLaren's fatal accident in June 1970, Hulme has led the McLaren team. He was Can-Am Champion in 1968 and 1970.

Underestimated by many people, Denny Hulme is among the world's very top drivers. With a competitive car he can lead anyone, as he proved in the opening race in the 1971 championship trail.

Grand Prix wins:

1967	*Monaco Grand Prix, Monte Carlo*	*Brabham Repco*
	German Grand Prix, Nürburgring	*Brabham Repco*
1968	*Italian Grand Prix, Monza*	*McLaren Ford*
	Canadian Grand Prix, St. Jovite	*McLaren Ford*
1969	*Mexican Grand Prix, Mexico City*	*McLaren Ford*

JACKY ICKX

Belgian, 6 Grand Prix wins
b January 1, 1945

The son of a motoring journalist, Jacky Ickx couldn't help but get involved in motor racing. His elder brother Pascal also raced. Jacky started with motorcycle trials at the age of sixteen, winning the national championship two years later. He overturned a BMW 700 in a hillclimb, but this did not stop Ford of Belgium from offering the young Ickx a Lotus Cortina for another hillclimb. He won and, at the age of eighteen, was offered a Ford contract.

In 1965 well-known talent-spotter Ken Tyrrell offered Ickx a Formula 3 drive for the following season. This soon led to Formula

2 and Ickx replaced the injured Pedro Rodriguez on the factory Cooper Maserati team in the 1967 Italian Grand Prix.

Ferrari signed up the young Belgian for 1968 and he won the French Grand Prix in the pouring rain. Surprisingly, he changed to the Brabham team for 1969 (mainly because of his Gulf fuel contract; Ferraris were on Shell) and won the German and Canadian Grands Prix.

Back to Ferrari for 1970, Ickx was a front-runner once initial teething problems with the Ferrari 312B had been overcome. He won the Austrian, Canadian and Mexican Grands Prix to be runner-up in the world championship to the late Jochen Rindt.

Grand Prix wins:

1968	*French Grand Prix, Rouen-les-Essarts*	*Ferrari*
1969	*German Grand Prix, Nürburgring*	*Brabham Ford*
	Canadian Grand Prix, Mosport Park	*Brabham Ford*
1970	*Austrian Grand Prix, Österreichring*	*Ferrari*
	Canadian Grand Prix, St. Jovite	*Ferrari*
	Mexican Grand Prix, Mexico City	*Ferrari*

INNES IRELAND

British, 1 Grand Prix win
b June 12, 1930

Innes Ireland, despite his name, is a Scot. To confuse matters even further, he once lived in Wales. At twenty-two he took part in his first race at Boreham in a 4½-liter Bentley; then a spell in the army meant no more racing until 1955.

After many successes with his own Lotus sports cars, Ireland was invited to join the Lotus Grand Prix team in 1959. In 1960 he led the Argentine Grand Prix in the first-ever rear-engined Lotus, the Climax-powered 18, but initial teething problems dropped him to sixth at the end. In 1961 he won the U.S. Grand Prix, despite an early spin, but was later dropped from the team. Thereafter he raced with occasional success for private teams such as UDT-Lay-

Ireland

McLaren

stall, British Racing Partnership, Reg Parnell Racing and Bernard White.

In his day Ireland could be up with the world's best; when not on form he trailed around at the rear, while he also had several spins and accidents. He retired from racing in 1967 and for a while was Sports Editor of *Autocar* magazine; his reports, like his driving, were either extremely good . . . or average.

Grand Prix win:
1961 U.S. Grand Prix, Watkins Glen   *Lotus Climax*

BRUCE McLAREN

New Zealander, 4 Grand Prix wins
b August 30, 1937; d June 2, 1970

Bruce McLaren was the youngest driver to have won a Grand Prix; aged twenty-two, he won the 1959 U.S. Grand Prix at Sebring in a factory Cooper Climax after his team leader, Jack Brabham, had broken down on the last lap.

Son of a garage owner, New Zealander McLaren first raced a 750cc Austin Ulster at the age of fourteen in 1952. In 1958 he

153

came to England on a "Driver-to-Europe Scholarship." By 1959 he was driving factory Formula 1 Coopers. He remained with Cooper until the end of 1965, from 1966 onward building and racing his own Grand Prix McLarens. In 1968 he won the Belgian Grand Prix, thereby joining Jack Brabham and Dan Gurney as constructor/ drivers who had won Grands Prix in their own machines.

McLaren was also a very successful sports car driver. He won the Le Mans 24-hours in 1966 driving a 7-liter Ford, and in 1967 and 1969 was Can-Am Champion with his own McLaren Chevrolet cars. Sadly, he was killed testing his latest Can-Am car at Goodwood in 1970 when the rear of the body came adrift, causing the car to veer out of control and smash into an obstruction.

Grand Prix wins:

1959 U.S. Grand Prix, Sebring	*Cooper Climax*
1960 Argentine Grand Prix, Buenos Aires	*Cooper Climax*
1962 Monaco Grand Prix, Monte Carlo	*Cooper Climax*
1968 Belgian Grand Prix, Francorchamps	*McLaren Ford*

STIRLING MOSS

British, 16 Grand Prix wins
b September 17, 1929

Stirling Moss never won a world championship. He was undoubtedly the best driver in the world from Fangio's retirement in mid-1958 until his accident in April 1962 which curtailed his racing career. Anyone who criticizes the world championship points scoring system cites Moss. He was runner-up in 1955, 1956, 1957 and 1958 and third in 1959, 1960 and 1961, mainly owing to inferior machinery or mechanical breakdowns, while his total of sixteen Grand Prix wins is bettered only by Jim Clark and Juan Manuel Fangio.

Moss was a "boy wonder" from the day he started competing in a 500cc Cooper in 1948 at the age of eighteen. In 1950 he was driving for the HWM Formula 2 team, scoring some excellent places with those underpowered machines. He also drove BRM, ERA,

Connaught and Cooper cars before deciding to go foreign in 1954. He bought a Maserati 250F Formula 1 car and the following year was number two to Fangio in the Mercedes-Benz équipe. He joined Maserati in 1956, then in 1957 Moss found that British cars were at last becoming competitive and joined the Vanwall team. Taking over Tony Brooks' car after his own had failed, Moss won the 1957 British Grand Prix at Aintree—the first world championship win for a British car.

Toward the end of his career Moss drove Cooper and Lotus cars for the British private entrant Rob Walker, for whom he notched up many notable wins. Perhaps the best was the 1958 Argentine Grand Prix when his tiny 170 bhp 2-liter Cooper Climax conquered the 280 bhp $2\frac{1}{2}$-liter Ferraris and Maseratis.

In sports car racing Moss was probably the greatest, even better than Fangio. In 1955 he won the Mille Miglia in a Mercedes-Benz 300SLR, being only the second non-Italian to do so out of twenty-four events.

Today Moss is involved in the promotion of motor racing: nine years after his Goodwood accident he is still as well-known as top active racing drivers.

155

Grand Prix wins:

1955	*British Grand Prix, Aintree*	*Mercedes-Benz*
1956	*Monaco Grand Prix, Monte Carlo*	*Maserati*
	Italian Grand Prix, Monza	*Maserati*
1957	*British Grand Prix, Aintree*	*Vanwall*
	(took over Brooks' car)	
	Pescara Grand Prix, Pescara	*Vanwall*
	Italian Grand Prix, Monza	*Vanwall*
1958	*Argentine Grand Prix, Buenos Aires*	*Cooper Climax*
	Dutch Grand Prix, Zandvoort	*Vanwall*
	Portuguese Grand Prix, Oporto	*Vanwall*
	Moroccan Grand Prix, Casablanca	*Vanwall*
1959	*Portuguese Grand Prix, Monsanto*	*Cooper Climax*
	Italian Grand Prix, Monza	*Cooper Climax*
1960	*Monaco Grand Prix, Monte Carlo*	*Lotus Climax*
	U.S. Grand Prix, Riverside	*Lotus Climax*
1961	*Monaco Grand Prix, Monte Carlo*	*Lotus Climax*
	German Grand Prix, Nürburgring	*Lotus Climax*

LUIGI MUSSO

Italian, 1 Grand Prix win
b 1924; d July 6, 1958

The nearest Luigi Musso ever came to a Grand Prix win was when Fangio took over his Ferrari to win the 1956 Argentine Grand Prix. Yet in the mid-1950s Musso was the best

156

Italian driver: he had five second places in Grand Prix racing, but no proper start-to-finish victory.

Musso, youngest of three brothers, whose father was a diplomat who spent many years in China, was deeply religious. His first race was the Tour of Sicily in 1950 in a 750cc Giannini sports car, but he crashed into a monument of Garibaldi and the car was never the same afterward. Later he drove Stanguellini and Maserati sports cars, to graduate to a Maserati 250F Formula 1 car in 1954. In 1956 he was on the Ferrari team, with which he remained until his fatal crash in the 1958 French Grand Prix at Reims. He made the fatal error of trying to take a 130-mph corner flat-out in his chase of winner Mike Hawthorn.

Grand Prix win:
1956 Argentine Grand Prix   *Ferrari*
     (car taken over by Fango)

GIAN-CLAUDIO REGAZZONI

Swiss, 1 Grand Prix win
b September 5, 1939

Born in Lugano, Switzerland, Gian-Claudio "Clay" Regazzoni lives in the Italian-language canton of Ticino and he spent much of his youth in northern Italy. He first raced a modified Simca and later an Abarth GT car. In 1964 he graduated to a Formula 3 Brabham, earning a reputation for being a very enthusiastic driver, and he found himself a place on the Tecno Formula 3 team.

By 1968 he was driving Tecno Formula 2 cars, putting up some impressive displays but not scoring any wins in this highly competitive form of racing. The following year he drove on the Ferrari Formula 2 team, but the cars were very disappointing and withdrawn before the season's close and Regazzoni went back to Tecno.

After some impressive test drives for Ferrari in 1969, Regazzoni was invited to drive on the Formula 1 team on occasions. On his first outing he was fourth in the Dutch Grand Prix, then fourth in

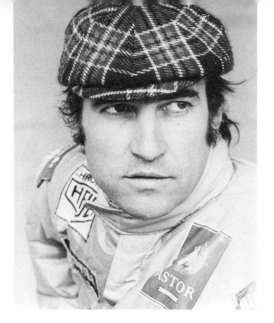

Regazzoni   **Rindt**

the British Grand Prix after a close battle with Denny Hulme's McLaren. This led to the Swiss driver's regular inclusion on the Formula 1 team and as his teammates Ickx and Giunti dropped out in the Italian Grand Prix at Monza with mechanical troubles, Regazzoni went on to score a well-judged and extremely popular victory.

For 1971 Regazzoni remains with Ferrari and despite his limited Formula 1 experience he is tipped as a potential World Champion.

Grand Prix win:
1970 Italian Grand Prix, Monza   *Ferrari*

JOCHEN RINDT

Austrian, 6 Grand Prix wins
b April 18, 1942; d September 5, 1970

Jochen Rindt's fatal accident while practicing for the 1970 Italian Grand Prix was one of motor racing's greatest tragedies. The Austrian was comfortably leading the world championship and as no one had surpassed his points total at the end of the year he was awarded the championship posthumously. His

158

Lotus 72 Ford suffered mechanical failure which sent it into the guardrail when braking from around 170 mph.

The son of a spice merchant, but orphaned when only a year old, Rindt was brought up by his grandparents. At twenty, he took part in his first race driving an Alfa Romeo saloon and by the following year, 1963, he was racing a Formula Junior Cooper Ford with tremendous verve and some success.

At Crystal Palace in 1964, driving a Formula 2 Brabham, Rindt shook the experts by dicing for the lead with Graham Hill and then going on to beat him. He had well and truly arrived and three months later drove a Formula 1 Brabham entered by Rob Walker in the Austrian Grand Prix.

He signed for Cooper in 1965, but the cars were not very competitive and for three years Rindt had to campaign with inferior machinery. Nevertheless, he still put up some fantastic drives—notably in the soaking wet 1966 Belgian Grand Prix—and continued to dominate Formula 2. In 1968 he changed to Brabham, the championship winners of 1966 and 1967, but that year was Brabham's blackest as the new Repco engine was both underpowered and unreliable.

It was not until Rindt signed with Lotus in 1969 that he had competitive Formula 1 machinery to drive. At first he did not see eye-to-eye with Lotus boss Colin Chapman, but at the end of the year he won the U.S. Grand Prix. The 1970 season saw Rindt and Lotus on top, first with a surprise win in the Monaco Grand Prix with an old Lotus 49C Ford and then with four consecutive victories with the revolutionary Lotus 72 Ford in Holland, France, Britain and Germany.

Grand Prix wins:

1969	*U.S. Grand Prix, Watkins Glen*	*Lotus Ford*
1970	*Monaco Grand Prix, Monte Carlo*	*Lotus Ford*
	Dutch Grand Prix, Zandvoort	*Lotus Ford*
	French Grand Prix, Clermont-Ferrand	*Lotus Ford*
	British Grand Prix, Brands Hatch	*Lotus Ford*
	German Grand Prix, Hockenheim	*Lotus Ford*

PEDRO RODRIGUEZ

Mexican, 2 Grand Prix wins
b January 18, 1940

Mexico's Pedro Rodriguez started riding motorcycles at the age of eleven, in 1951. He won his first motorcycle championship three years later and in 1955 was driving cars. At the age of eighteen he drove in the Le Mans 24-hours in 1958 and co-drove with his younger brother Ricardo the following year.

Rodriguez almost retired from racing at the end of 1962 when Ricardo was killed practicing for the Mexican Grand Prix. But he returned early in 1963 to win the 500-kilometer sports car race at Daytona. Although he had a few "guest" outings for Lotus and Ferrari, Rodriguez did not find a regular Grand Prix drive until 1967 when he drove for the Cooper Maserati team. He won first time out in South Africa.

He signed for BRM in 1968, then drove a privately entered BRM and a works Ferrari in 1969. Back to BRM in 1970 he won the Belgian Grand Prix after a display of brilliance around the ultra-fast and dangerous Francorchamps circuit. But for a last-minute stop for fuel, he would probably have won the U.S. Grand Prix as well.

Rodriguez is also a very talented sports car driver, having won almost every major long-distance event in the calendar.

Grand Prix wins:
1967 South African Grand Prix, Kyalami   Cooper Maserati
1970 Belgian Grand Prix, Francorchamps   BRM

160

LUDOVICO SCARFIOTTI

Italian, 1 Grand Prix win
b October 18, 1933; d June 8, 1968

Ludovico Scarfiotti was a great all-rounder, being at home in a short hillclimb, a 24-hour sports car race or a Formula 1 event. Son of a cement manufacturer (his grandfather was the first president of Fiat), Scarfiotti first raced at twenty-two in a Fiat 1100. After some good drives for Osca in Formula Junior and sports car races, he got his first drive for Ferrari as early as 1960 driving sports cars.

His first experience in Formula 1 racing was in 1963, when he replaced the injured Willy Mairesse on the Ferrari team, but he crashed practicing for the French Grand Prix and supposedly retired from motor racing. He was soon back again and drove Formula 1 Ferraris in 1966, winning the Italian Grand Prix. But following fellow-countryman Bandini's fatal accident at Monaco, Scarfiotti retired again in 1967. He returned yet again in 1968, driving Cooper BRM Formula 1 cars and Porsche sports machinery.

Practicing for the Rossfeld hillclimb in Germany, Scarfiotti's factory Porsche plunged off the road into some trees. He suffered severe skull injuries and died in the hospital.

Grand Prix win:
1966 Italian Grand Prix, Monza   *Ferrari*

JO SIFFERT

Swiss, 1 Grand Prix win
b July 7, 1936

Jo Siffert comes from a poor family; at one time he had to pick flowers to make enough money to exist. In 1957, aged twenty-one, he managed to find enough money to go motorcycle racing; two years later he was Swiss champion.

In 1960 he started racing a Formula Junior Stanguellini, but changed to a more competitive Lotus in 1961. He won several European races and drove an uncompetitive Formula 1 Lotus Climax the following year. In 1963 Siffert took the plunge and bought his own Lotus 24 BRM Formula 1 car, changing to a Brabham BT11 BRM the following season. He beat many top names in the 1964 Mediterranean Grand Prix at Enna in Sicily and repeated his victory the following year, this time as a member of Rob Walker's Formula 1 team.

Siffert remained with Walker until the end of 1969. He won the British Grand Prix at Brands Hatch in 1968 after a really superb drive in a brand new Lotus 49B Ford, but 1969 was punctuated by a few accidents. In 1970 he drove a factory Formula 1 car for the first time, a March 701 Ford, but he was never really happy with the car and was pleased to sign with BRM for 1971.

In sports car racing Siffert has enjoyed many victories, while he also has several Formula 2 victories to his credit.

Grand Prix win:
1968 British Grand Prix, Brands Hatch   *Lotus Ford*

JACKIE STEWART

British, 12 Grand Prix wins
World Champion 1969
b June 11, 1939

Younger brother of Ecurie Ecosse driver Jimmy Stewart, Jackie worked in the family garage in Dunbartonshire, Scotland, after he left school. In 1961 he had his first race and two years later he was driving for the Ecurie Ecosse team too. Word soon spread south about the skill of this unknown Scotsman and Ken Tyrrell included him in his Formula 3 team of 1964.

By the end of the year Stewart had received several Formula 1 offers! In the Formula 3 Cooper BMC he won first time out at Snetterton in the rain and continued the winning streak until the end of the year. For 1965 Stewart signed with BRM and in his first year of Formula 1 racing he won the Italian Grand Prix. The next two years were not so good as BRM did not have a fully competitive Formula 1 car; he also had a serious accident in the 1966 Belgian Grand Prix which put him out of racing for a few weeks.

For 1968 Ken Tyrrell decided to run his own Formula 1 team and Stewart rejoined his old équipe. Driving a Ford-engined Matra MS10, Stewart was handicapped by a wrist injury during the early part of the year (he missed two races) but scored wins in Holland, Germany and the United States and almost stole the championship from Graham Hill. In 1969 he made no mistakes and won six of the season's eleven races to be undisputed champion.

With Matra deciding to use their own V12 engine in 1970 and Stewart's allegiance to Ford, Tyrrell ran Ford-engined Marches in

163

1970 and later built a car of his own. It was not Stewart's year: after an early-season win in Spain the opposition proved too good, although the Tyrrell showed immense promise at the end of the year, if not reliability.

With Jochen Rindt's death in late 1970, Stewart is currently considered to be the best driver in the world.

Grand Prix wins:

1965	*Italian Grand Prix, Monza*	*BRM*
1966	*Monaco Grand Prix, Monte Carlo*	*BRM*
1968	*Dutch Grand Prix, Zandvoort*	*Matra Ford*
	German Grand Prix, Nürburgring	*Matra Ford*
	U.S. Grand Prix, Watkins Glen	*Matra Ford*
1969	*South African Grand Prix, Kyalami*	*Matra Ford*
	Spanish Grand Prix, Montjuich Park	*Matra Ford*
	Dutch Grand Prix, Zandvoort	*Matra Ford*
	French Grand Prix, Clermont-Ferrand	*Matra Ford*
	British Grand Prix, Silverstone	*Matra Ford*
	Italian Grand Prix, Monza	*Matra Ford*
1970	*Spanish Grand Prix, Jarama*	*March Ford*

JOHN SURTEES

British, 6 Grand Prix wins
World Champion 1964
b February 11, 1934

John Surtees was a World Champion motorcyclist before he switched to racing cars. Son of a garage owner and motorcyclist, Surtees started his competition career in his father's sidecar in 1949. His first solo motorcycle race was in 1951, when he was seventeen, and the first of his seven world titles on two wheels was in 1956.

Surtees turned to motor cars in 1960, alternating with racing motorcycles for the first year. His first race was in a Formula Junior Cooper BMC, but in a little over a month he had graduated via Formula 2 to Formula 1 with Team Lotus. He was second in the

164

British Grand Prix and led the Portuguese Grand Prix until he had an accident.

After an unsuccessful two years with the Yeoman Credit/Bowmaker team racing Coopers and Lolas, Surtees joined Ferrari in 1963. He won the world championship in 1964 in a photo-finish with Graham Hill and Jim Clark. In 1966, driving a Lola T70 Chevrolet, Surtees won the first Can-Am championship—a year after a serious crash driving the same type of machine in Canada.

Midway through 1966 Surtees had a disagreement with Ferrari and quit the team, racing Cooper Maseratis for the remainder of the year. In 1967 and 1968 he drove for Honda, then in 1969 for BRM, but he encountered difficulties with both teams. In 1970 he went on his own, racing a McLaren until his own Surtees Formula 1 car was complete. Immediately his old form returned and today Surtees must always be included on the list of potential winners of any race.

Grand Prix wins:

1963	*German Grand Prix, Nürburgring*	*Ferrari*
1964	*German Grand Prix, Nürburgring*	*Ferrari*
	Italian Grand Prix, Monza	*Ferrari*
1966	*Belgian Grand Prix, Francorchamps*	*Ferrari*
	Mexican Grand Prix, Mexico City	*Cooper Maserati*
1967	*Italian Grand Prix, Monza*	*Honda*

Stewart   **Surtees**

PIERO TARUFFI

Italian, 1 Grand Prix win
b October 12, 1906

Piero Taruffi's greatest win was not in Grand Prix racing: it was his last-ever race, the Mille Miglia sports car event. He won it on his thirteenth attempt driving a factory Ferrari in 1957, the last occasion when this event was a pure road race. Taruffi was fifty.

He won a touring car race in 1924 at the age of seventeen driving the family Fiat, with his father, sister and a distinguished surgeon as passengers. During his career he drove many of the world's leading cars, including Alfa Romeo, Bugatti, ERA, Maserati, Ferrari, Mercedes-Benz and Lancia. In Grand Prix racing his best years were with Ferrari in the early 1950s. He scored his one Grand Prix victory in 1952.

Taruffi is also renowned as a motorcycle engineer and designer and a record-breaker.

Grand Prix win:
1952 Swiss Grand Prix, Bremgarten   *Ferrari*

MAURICE TRINTIGNANT

French, 2 Grand Prix wins
b October 30, 1917

Maurice Trintignant got his taste for motor racing at the age of twelve—as a riding mechanic in his two elder brothers' Bugattis. In 1933 one of them, René, was killed after crashing to avoid a policeman who suddenly stepped onto the race track. The car was rebuilt and five years later Maurice bought it to start racing himself.

After the war he raced the Bugatti and an Amilcar before joining the Gordini team. In 1954 he joined Ferrari, for whom he won the Monaco Grand Prix the following year, and in 1956 he was a member of the British Vanwall team. He also drove the new Bugatti T251 that year in the French Grand Prix, but it was a failure and never raced again.

Trintignant raced privately entered Coopers in the late 1950s and early 1960s and ran his own BRM in 1964, his last active year in motor racing before he retired to run his vineyard in southern France. At one time he was mayor of his hometown.

Grand Prix wins:
1955 Monaco Grand Prix, Monte Carlo　　　　　*Ferrari*
1958 Monaco Grand Prix, Monte Carlo　　　　　*Cooper Climax*

WOLFGANG VON TRIPS

German, 2 Grand Prix wins
b May 4, 1928; d September 10, 1961

The only German driver to have won a Grand Prix since the world championship was inaugurated in 1950, nobleman Wolfgang von Trips was killed at Monza in 1961 when in a position to win the world championship. He was recovering from a slow start when on the second lap his Ferrari hit Jim Clark's Lotus. The Lotus spun harmlessly, but the Ferrari sliced into the spectators and claimed a dozen victims, including von Trips himself.

In his early days, driving Porsche, Mercedes-Benz and Ferrari sports cars, von Trips had a tremendous reputation as an accident looking for somewhere to happen. But he matured into a more sensible driver when he became a regular member of the Grand Prix "circus."

The Italian Grand Prix at Monza was one of his most unlucky events, for he crashed in practice for the 1956 race, crashed on the first lap of the 1958 event and was killed in 1961.

Grand Prix wins:
1961 Dutch Grand Prix, Zandvoort   *Ferrari*
      British Grand Prix, Aintree   *Ferrari*

WORLD CHAMPIONS

1950	Guiseppe "Nino" Farina, Italy	Alfa Romeo
1951	Juan Manuel Fangio, Argentina	Alfa Romeo
1952	Alberto Ascari, Italy	Ferrari
1953	Alberto Ascari, Italy	Ferrari
1954	Juan Manuel Fangio, Argentina	Maserati, Mercedes
1955	Juan Manuel Fangio, Argentina	Mercedes
1956	Juan Manuel Fangio, Argentina	Ferrari
1957	Juan Manuel Fangio, Argentina	Maserati
1958	Mike Hawthorn, England	Ferrari
1959	Jack Brabham, Australia	Cooper
1960	Jack Brabham, Australia	Cooper
1961	Phil Hill, U.S.A.	Ferrari
1962	Graham Hill, England	BRM
1963	Jim Clark, Scotland	Lotus
1964	John Surtees, England	Ferrari
1965	Jim Clark, Scotland	Lotus
1966	Jack Brabham, Australia	Brabham
1967	Denis Hulme, New Zealand	Brabham
1968	Graham Hill, England	Lotus
1969	Jackie Stewart, Scotland	Matra
1970	Jochen Rindt, Austria	Lotus

GLOSSARY

Backmarker: Driver at the tail of the field, usually slower than the leaders.

Banking: Inward inclination of corners of an oval or circular race track.

Can-Am: The Canadian-American Championship for drivers of sports/racing cars.

Chassis: 1. Underpart of an automobile, consisting of frame with axles, brakes, wheels, engine, transmission, driveline and exhaust system. 2. Frame only without running gear.

Chicane: Obstacles or barriers added to existing road course to form a tighter turn or series of turns, generally with the objective of reducing average speed or speed through a certain section.

Circuit: Road course used for conducting automobile races, on which cars repeatedly retrace the same route.

Club Meeting: Automobile competition organized by a club for its members and guests. Indicates an amateur event.

Dicing: Close, exciting and highly competitive driving.

Drafting: See Slipstreaming.

Factory: A factory car is one owned and entered for a race or rally by its manufacturer. A factory team is one run by the manufacturer.

FIA: Fédération Internationale de l'Automobile. International automotive governing body.

Formula 1: (1966-1975) FIA competition category describing Grand Prix championship cars. Up to 3000cc, unsupercharged. Minimum dry weight without ballast, 500 kilograms. Commercial fuel. Self-starter obligatory. No oil replenishment allowed during race.

Formula 2: (1967-1971) FIA competition category. 1600cc unsupercharged. Maximum cylinders: 6. Block from production car. Commercial fuel. Minimum dry weight without ballast, 420 kilograms.

Formula 3: FIA competition category providing for competition within the means of private entrants intended to serve as a training ground for future Grand Prix drivers and development of production engines and components.

GP (Grand Prix): From the French usage. 1. Race for Formula 1 cars. 2. Designation of a major international road racing event.

GPDA: Grand Prix Drivers Association.

Guardrail: Metal barrier placed around the circuit to prevent cars leaving the track in case of an accident and to protect the spectators.

Hairpin: Acute corner on road racing circuit.

Lap(s): Complete tour(s) of the race course, track or circuit.

Lap of Honor: Parade lap for the winner of a race after the presentation of an award or trophy.

Line: 1. The fastest path around a given race course, e.g. the correct line or the best line. 2. The path being followed at any moment by a racing car and driver.

Liter: Metric unit of volumetric measure, 1000 cubic centimeters. Equivalent to 61 cubic inches.

Marshal: Flagman or communications worker.

Monocoque: Design which unitizes body and chassis into single structure.

Paddock: Area, generally adjacent to pits, where competition cars and service vehicles are parked, serviced and prepared.

Pit(s): Service stall or area assigned to each car competing in a race.

Pit Lane: Lane in front of pits for entrance and exit of racing cars.

Pit Stop: Stop made at pit by competing car.

Pole Position: The most advantageous position on the starting grid, usually reserved for the fastest driver in practice.

Qualifying: Prerace speed trials held to determine eligibility for an event and/or order of cars and drivers for the start.

Roadholding: Car's ability to grip the road during cornering.

Scrutineering: Detailed technical inspection to assess raceworthiness or conformity of competing cars to regulations.

Scuderia: (Italian) Team, e.g. Scuderia Ferrari.

Shunt: Accident, involving crash.

Slipstreaming: Driving very close to tail of another racing car to take advantage of resulting decreased wind resistance.

Space-frame: Chassis frame built of multiple tubes.

Starter: Marshal who controls the master flag at the start/finish line. The chief starter.

Start/Finish: The line that serves (in nearly all cases) as the place on the circuit where a race starts and finishes.

Starting Grid: Area where races are started. Cars are usually lined up in a pre-determined pattern, such as 2-2-2, 3-2-3, 4-3-4, 3-3-3, etc., formation.

Tech Inspection: See Scrutineering.

Warmup Lap: Lap prior to the start of a race.

INDEX

175

177

178